The Epoch of
Napoleon

The Epoch of
Napoleon

OWEN CONNELLY
University of South Carolina

Holt, Rinehart and Winston, Inc.
New York   Chicago   San Francisco   Atlanta
Dallas   Montreal   Toronto   London   Sydney

The map on page 63 is from *The Napoleonic Era in Europe* by Jacques Godechot, Beatrice F. Hyslop and David L. Dowd. Copyright © 1971 by Holt, Rinehart and Winston, Inc. Reproduced by permission of Holt, Rinehart and Winston, Inc.

Preface

THIS book is designed to present, in capsule form, but without sacrifice of color, the essential facts about Napoleon Bonaparte and France, Europe, and the world in the Napoleonic era. Chapters 1, 2, 4, and 7 constitute a narrative history of the period. Chapters 3, 5, and 6 are topical, and add detail on matters merely mentioned elsewhere. Each set is complete in itself, though the beginning student, for best understanding, should read all chapters in proper sequence.

Unlike most short "Napoleon books," this one is not biography or military, political, and/or diplomatic history. It has elements of all of these. The emphasis, however, is on Napoleon as civil executive in France and Europe. More information on his legal, institutional, educational, social, and other reforms is presented here than in any other volume of this size. The book deals with his work and that of his enlightened proconsuls in the kingdoms and lesser states he created—from Spain to the Grand Duchy of Warsaw. It describes the progressive changes he promoted or provoked in allied and enemy states. It also covers the effects of his domination of Europe on the United States, Latin America, the Middle East, Africa, India, and the Indies. Much of the material included can be found elsewhere only in specialized studies, many in foreign languages.

The Introduction raises questions regarding the "Napoleonic Legend." The Conclusions discuss the real Napoleon, present a thesis on his "Grand Design," and speculate as to its impact, had it been achieved, on world history. Throughout, the effects of his work which are still apparent today are highlighted.

If it has been properly done, this little book will be of value to students who want the "word" on Napoleon—fast and in plain English. Sections of the text should serve also, with the bibliographical essay, as starting points for those interested in investigating particular subjects, be they Napoleonic Holland or Frankfurt, Napoleon's battle tactics or colonial schemes, or the man himself.

Columbia, S.C.   O. C.
January 1972

Contents

*The Imperial Guard always marched
to the Marseillaise.*
—Napoleon at Saint Helena

Introduction

EXILED on Saint Helena, the cancer that would kill him eating at his entrails, Napoleon read a flood of literature picturing him as a war-mad tyrant with the blood of thousands on his hands. He raged, he wept, he rationalized that "martyrdom" would guarantee his fame. But mostly he fought, this time with words, interpreting his career for Emmanuel de Las Cases, Generals Charles Montholon and Henri Bertrand, the Irish surgeon Barry O'Meara, and other companions. His auditors published. They were applauded; they were attacked. Memoirists, historians, novelists, and poets joined the fight. A war-of-the-books ensued, which, twenty years after his death, Napoleon seemed to have won, hands down.

In 1840 the French public, restive and bored under the "bourgeois monarchy" of Louis Philippe, hungry for a taste of past glory, demanded the return of the emperor's remains to France. Britain consented. The world press roared approval. The banks of the Seine, Victor Hugo wrote, were "black with people" as the funeral barge moved to Paris. When the casket was borne into the Invalides, a chamberlain intoned "L'Empereur," as if Napoleon were alive. Spectators wept and the king of the French and his entourage stood, hatless and bowed, to receive the hero.

But historians questioned if Napoleon had been enshrined on the basis of his real accomplishments. Had he not begun the building of a legend of himself at Saint Helena? Nay, had he not earlier dramatized his whole career in his bulletins and pronouncements and through writers, poets, painters—even musicians—in his pay? In 1969, the bicentennial of his birth, a display was formed in the French National Library to prove just that. An acute American observer, Hans J. Morgenthau, recorded his reaction:

> Yet while this exhibition reveals the dissembler, the manipulator in Napoleon, it also brings out, almost *malgré elle,* what other exhibitions are meant to make visible: his incomparable greatness. . . . Take away the parades, the pseudo-religious fanaticism, the totalitarian re-integration of a disintegrating society, and what is left of Hitler? A destructive maniac. . . . Take away the artifices of the Napoleonic legend, and what is left is the greatest man of action the western world has seen.[1]

Napoleon purported to believe that history would grant him glory. "Posterity," he told Las Cases, "will judge only by the facts." But he also said that Waterloo would eclipse all his victories. For what, then, did he expect to be remembered? Perhaps the answer is in the letter he dictated on his deathbed for his son, whom he hoped would one day be emperor.

> I have given the prime example of a government which favored the interests of all. I did not govern for the nobles, the priests, the middle class, or the workers. I governed for . . . the whole great French family. . . .

---

[1] *New York Review,* XVI (26 February 1970), 38 ff. Reprinted with permission from *The New York Review of Books.* Copyright © 1970, New York Review, Inc.

Regenerate [Europe] . . . through laws; establish above all institutions which destroy all traces of feudalism, which assure the dignity of man [and] develop the germs of prosperity which have lain dormant over the centuries; see that the masses share in that which is today the province of the few; reunite Europe through indissoluble federative ties. . . .

The "martyred" emperor's son was destined to die young. His mantle would fall to his curious nephew, Napoleon III. But the question is: Did Napoleon rule as he advised his son to rule? His military genius, which he was at pains not to defend, is denied by very few. The record is too overwhelming. For the rest, to what extent did Napoleon rule for all the French people? What claim does he have to having tried to regenerate the European peoples and unite them in a viable political federation?

It is the last two questions which this book will try to answer. Attention will perforce be given to Napoleon's origins and life, and to his campaigns. But it is his nonmilitary career that will be emphasized.

CHAPTER ONE

Buonaparte

> *I want my remains to rest on the banks of the Seine,*
> *among the French people I have loved so much . . .*
> —Napoleon at Saint Helena

ORIGINS   It is ironic that France's greatest hero—
"the Little Corporal," the Emperor—France's Alexander, its Caesar—was born Napoleone Buonaparte,
of a proudly Italian family, and in Corsica, which
had been French for only a few months.

In 1768 Genoa, unable to put down a movement for the independence of Corsica led by Pasquale Paoli, sold the island to Louis XV. French
troops crushed the rebellion; Paoli fled to England.
Most of his followers accepted the French king's
amnesty, among them Carlo (Charles) Buonaparte,
age twenty-two, who returned home to Ajaccio with
his wife, Letizia Ramolina, and their baby son,
Giuseppe (Joseph). On August 15, 1769, their second
son, Napoleone, was born.

The Buonapartes were of Florentine nobility;
Carlo entered the French aristocracy as a count.

The first Buonaparte had come to Corsica in 1567 in the service of Genoa; the Ramolinos, Italian gentry, a little later. Both families were coastal people, considered semiforeign by the "real" Corsicans of the wild interior uplands. These were the descendants of successive waves of conquerors—Etruscans, Phoenicians, Romans, Byzantine Greeks, Vandals, Goths, Saracen Turks, Berber and Moorish pirates—and finally Italians. Proud, independent, Spartan in habit, Christian by religion, they settled their differences by the vendetta—each clan avenging its own. Of 130 murderers arrested in 1769, only one was convicted in the French courts. Coastal and mountain people remained communities apart. Only men with family ties to both groups, like Paoli, could unite them.

The Buonapartes had some connections with the mountaineers, but they had consistently—until Carlo's time—served Genoa, considered themselves Italians, and educated their sons in Italy. The family had never produced a professional soldier. Most had been lawyers, judges, officials, or churchmen—members of the largely Italian "establishment."

Carlo Buonaparte was slender, handsome, sandy-haired and blue-eyed, bright, charming, a *bella figura,* always fashionably dressed. No man for lost causes, he quickly offered his services to the French governor, the Count de Marbeuf, who gratefully accepted. A noble with a law degree from Pisa and widely acquainted with the "right people," he was extremely useful to the new rulers. By the time of his premature death in 1785 at the age of thirty-nine,[1] he was one of the most important men on the island—crown judicial officer and past secretary of the Estates—and known at the court of Louis XVI, where he had often represented Corsican, and his own, interests. He was a past master at securing scholarships for his children from crown and church.

Letizia Ramolino had married Carlo at fourteen. Velvet-eyed, dark-haired, with strong classic features and a brilliant smile—all the more devastating for its infrequent use—"My mother," Napoleon remembered "was as beautiful as love." She

---

[1] Of stomach cancer.

both graced island society and delighted the clergy; all her life she attended mass daily. And she also ran the Buonaparte farms and mill for Carlo, a poor manager, and governed the household with an iron hand. She gave her husband eight children—five boys and three girls—Joseph, Napoleon, Lucien, Louis, Jerome, Elisa, Pauline, and Caroline.[2] She was left a widow at thirty-five, but managed, with Joseph's help, to care for the family until Napoleon rose to fame. Throughout her life she remained handsome and dignified, and as Madame Mère of the emperor impressed the courts of Europe with her stoic serenity, which broke only after Napoleon's death at Saint Helena. She outlived him by fifteen years.

Casa Buonaparte in Ajaccio was large—4 floors, 20 rooms —but extremely bare. Letizia, once asked if, as a child, Napoleon really drew military diagrams on her rugs, laughed and replied: "We had no rugs in Corsica." The Buonapartes' food was simple, their clothes, except Carlo's, homemade from homespun fabrics, their luxuries very few. Ajaccio was a "city" of 3000; the family was supported by its farms and mill. Napoleon's later legendary stamina surely owed much to the fact that he was a country boy. He and Joseph roamed the hills, swam in the sea, climbed trees, rode horses, and sometimes played at working in the fields.

For the first six years of Napoleon's life he and Joseph were the only children in the house. Joseph, the first child, was the heir, the good little boy, blessed with his father's looks, big blue eyes, and an ability to please. Napoleon, less attractive and taken for granted, fought for attention. He was belligerent, demanding, loud, and willful. He picked fights with Joseph as soon as he could stand—for reasons his brother never understood. Joseph was a model student, with better grades then Napoleon except in math. Napoleon was a terror, even beating up little girls in primary school. Joseph remained everyone's favorite. Although Napoleon came to respect Joseph's gentle qualities, and later loaded him with honors, he never forgot their child-

[2] The baptismal names of the brothers were Giuseppe, Lucciano, Luigi, and Girolamo; the girls Maria Anna, Maria Paola, and Maria Annunziata. Four other children died in infancy.

hood relationship. He saw to it that Joseph never became, as Miot de Melito put it, a "rival personality."

From Letizia, Napoleon learned discipline, perseverance, economy to the point of parsimony, and devotion to family. From Carlo he got a sense of elegance, style—go hungry if necessary, but never be without a good suit—and charm, which Napoleon had in abundance, when he chose to use it. Doubtless, also, Carlo's opportunism rubbed off on him, together with a lawyer's ability to "present his case." He inherited also a robust constitution and good looks, though he was less handsome than Joseph or Jerome. The Italian sculptor Antonio Canova remarked on the perfect proportions of his body. Especially when he was a young hero, painters never tired of picturing the strong face and arresting blue-gray eyes; few, unfortunately, caught his infectious smile which so many intimates describe.

FRENCH SCHOOLING   In December 1778 Carlo took his eldest sons to the Oratorian college of Autun, where they took a "cram course" in French.[3] Joseph remained there to train for the church (which he later abandoned for the law). Napoleon, after three months, went on to military school at Brienne on a more prestigious royal scholarship. Still, Joseph was the favored one; with his talent, he was expected one day to be a bishop—honored, secure, and with a good income. Carlo had not chosen Napoleon for Brienne because he showed the most promise. He was bright, but had always been a disciplinary problem. The family had to find a career for its "little wolf." The military profession seemed suitable, though neither the army nor the navy, preferred at first, offered great opportunities. The pay was low; as a sublieutenant, Napoleon made about $18.50 a month. Moreover, a child of minor, "foreign" nobility could not aspire to high rank. He was likely to retire as a captain or major.

At Brienne, Napoleon was the favorite neither of his teachers nor of the students. The latter made fun of his name, appearance, and Corsican accent. He was a fighter, so the mock-

---

[3] Here they changed their first names: Napoleone became Napoleon; Giuseppe, Joseph. Buonaparte remained the family name, however, until much later.

Napoleon at the military school in Brienne. This artist's conception conveys the attitude of many of his French schoolmates toward the little "Italian." *(The New York Public Library)*

ery went on mostly behind his back. But it hurt. He struck back with diatribes about freeing his homeland from the French oppressors. Paoli was his hero. In playground "wars" he became a leader, but after school hours he was a lonely little boy. He devoted himself to his books, and made a good record. In 1784, because of his ability in math, he was sent to finish his schooling at the École Militaire, in Paris. This was the "school of future generals," which admitted largely sons of the highest nobility.

As a scholarship student, however, Napoleon suffered few slights. His French had improved and the royal allowance was more generous, so he lived in the same style as the others. He exerted himself to make friends and prudently stopped talking of Corsican independence.

He was commissioned (1785) after one year. This, however, was no extraordinary feat; he had completed most of his training at Brienne. He was only sixteen, but some of his classmates were younger. And he was not the top student. He ranked forty-second in a class of fifty-eight. Nevertheless he got a good assignment—to the artillery. His mathematical skill was a factor, but another was that artillerymen, though elite specialists, were expected to remain just that. Officers destined to command armies normally were commissioned in the infantry or cavalry.

INTELLECTUAL DEVELOPMENT For seven years (1785–1792), Napoleon was a poverty-stricken lieutenant. He took most of his leave—29 months in all—in Corsica, where room and board were free. What little money he could save went largely for books. He read widely—Plato, Aristotle, Thucydides, Mohammed, histories of all kinds, Fielding's *Tom Jones,* in translation, the classic French playwrights, and the works of the *philosophes.*

Few teachers seem to have influenced him markedly, save perhaps the Marshal du Teil at the artillery school at Auxonne, where he studied briefly. In broader military matters he educated himself, reading and making copious notes, still extant, on the campaigns of Alexander the Great, Caesar, Frederick the Great, Marlborough, Turenne, the Great Condé—and of course Charlemagne, who particularly caught his imagination.

The aspect of Enlightenment thought that influenced him

most was surely the authoritarian undercurrent in the works of Montesquieu, Voltaire, and Rousseau, among others. None of them had great faith in the common man. Rousseau preached government by the "general will," which seems democratic, but he defined it as what was best for the people, whether they approved or not. Thus the men of the Terror, following Rousseau, considered themselves democrats because they saw themselves as governing for the people. Napoleon later expressed similar sentiments: "Sovereignty resides in the French people, in the sense that everything without exception ought to be done in their interest, for their welfare and for their glory."

Enlightenment sentiment in France had been, in fact, in line with the French tradition of government by intelligent authority. Only the standard had changed; authority—the "qualified"—had to be "enlightened." Napoleon was in full accord.

CORSICA AGAIN   As late as 1789 Napoleon still thought of Corsican independence. When the National Assembly converted the island from crown colony to a province of France, however, his loyalty to France increased. And when, in 1790, Pasquale Paoli was returned to Corsica as royal governor, he was fully converted. Yet when Lieutenant Buonaparte, while on leave, met "the Babbo,"[4] he was disillusioned at his conservatism; Paoli, for his part, judged Napoleon an egotistic "intriguer." The governor promoted Joseph's political career and made Lucien his secretary, but ignored "that little lieutenant."

Nevertheless, by devious means, Napoleon got himself elected lieutenant colonel in the Corsican national guard. Paoli, at the first excuse, dispatched him to France. It proved a favor. For overstaying his leave, he had lost his regular commission; but France was now at war, officers scarce, so he got it back, with promotion to captain. He was in Paris on August 10, 1792, and watched as the mobs swept into the Tuileries, slaughtering the Swiss Guards, who were without orders. "If Louis XVI had mounted his horse," he wrote Joseph, "the victory would have been his." Thereafter he sided with the republicans of the Convention, and shortly was a Jacobin.

---

[4] "Old Papa," a term of affection.

But better a colonel than a captain. He returned to Corsica in the fall to take part, as a Guard officer, in an expedition against Sardinia, which failed miserably. Paoli relieved him of all command. He and Lucien took to organizing the Jacobins in Corsica and establishing liaison with clubs in France. Paoli, in control of the mass of the population—the mountaineers—began establishing contacts with the British.

In January 1793, when the Convention sent Louis XVI to the guillotine, "the Babbo" was horrified. Barbarians! "They have killed their king, the best of men!" Lucien made for France, where he denounced Paoli as a traitor before the Jacobin clubs of Toulon and Marseilles. "The Babbo" called an assembly which declared independence and outlawed the Buonapartes and other Francophiles. The family fled to France in June 1793. Joseph settled them near Marseilles. Napoleon went back to the army. Finally, and irrevocably, he was altogether a Frenchman.

TOULON Napoleon was a product of the Revolution, but more specifically of the Terror. Maximilien Robespierre took over the Committee of Public Safety shortly after the Buonapartes reached France. He had an ardent supporter in Napoleon, whose "Souper de Beaucaire" has survived to prove it.[5] It was the Terrorist Christophe Saliceti, a Corsican, who gave Napoleon his first major opportunity as a soldier.

That opportunity came at Toulon, which revolted against the government in June 1793 in protest against the expulsion of the moderate Girondins from the Convention. The rebels were supported by a British fleet and a few British, Spanish, and Neapolitan troops. The city was besieged by a French army, accompanied by civilian "watchdogs." One of these was Saliceti.

When the artillery commander, General Dommartin, was wounded, Saliceti brought in Captain Buonaparte, who was nearby, to replace him. Napoleon fixed on Fort Éguillette, on a western promontory overlooking the harbor, as the key to victory. From there, he believed, his artillery could fire directly

---

[5] "Supper at Beaucaire" (1793), a pamphlet, recounts an imaginary conversation at table at an inn. A "young officer" refutes the anti-Jacobin arguments of four conservative "Federalist" businessmen.

on the British fleet in the harbor. The fort was taken and he proved right. No sooner had the newly emplaced artillery begun firing than the British fleet withdrew, taking the troops with it (December 18, 1793). Toulon soon fell.

Praised to the sky by Saliceti, echoed by other representatives-on-mission to the army, including Paul Barras, Napoleon got unusual recognition in the military dispatches. At the end of December Captain Buonaparte, just twenty-four, was promoted to brigadier general. France, meanwhile, was under attack by all Europe, save Russia, and Britain.

CARNOT How unusual was Napoleon's case? Not very. Lazare Carnot, the military member of the Committee of Public Safety, the "architect of victory," a lean, horse-faced former captain of engineers, had set out to purge the officer corps. He had already set in motion the *levée en masse*—mass draft—which was producing armies larger than any ever seen in Europe before. He was systematically eliminating older officers, incompetents, and real or suspected royalists and elevating younger men who had proved themselves on the battlefield. The same year Napoleon was promoted, eight of his future marshals got equal or higher rank. Among these were Louis Nicolas Davout, twenty-three, Jean Baptiste Jourdan, André Masséna, and Pierre Augereau. The average age of the new generals was thirty-two.

FUTURE UNCERTAIN Assigned to the staff of the Army of Italy, Napoleon remained in the south of France. Joseph, meanwhile, became acquainted with the affluent Clary family of Marseilles. In 1794 he married Julie Clary and was taken into the family's commercial business. This helped him support his mother and the five children still at home. Napoleon fell in love with the very young and frivolous Désirée Clary, who later married Marshal Bernadotte and became queen of Sweden. She seems to have found the little general merely amusing—though she later said otherwise. When he left, she did not bother to write. "The silent one," Napoleon called her plaintively in a letter to Joseph.

In July 1794 Robespierre went to the guillotine. All over France his followers were arrested, among them Napoleon. He was freed within two weeks, however, since little could be produced to show that he had been more than a military man taking orders. He was shortly transferred to Paris and offered command of an infantry brigade in the Vendée. Command infantry against a rabble of royalist guerrillas? Never. Where was the glory? He refused and lost his commission. Saliceti and Paul Barras, however, got his rank restored. Both had turned against Robespierre in time to remain in the Convention. Napoleon was available, therefore, in Paris, where there was a crisis of government in October 1795.

THE CONVENTION AND PARIS   After the fall of Robespierre, the Convention had returned to its original task: writing a new constitution. By the end of September 1795 it was finished and French voters had approved it, but not Paris. The Parisians suffered from hunger and unemployment, which they blamed on the repeal by the Convention of the price and wage controls of the Terror. Actually poor crops and the hard winter of 1794–1795 had more to do with their troubles. But they feared the new government—the Directory—would make matters worse. In their desperation they turned to royalist leaders who promised them relief. It was planned to march on the Convention, sitting in the Tuileries, destroy it, and the constitution with it. Afterward? Who knew?

The Convention put Paul Barras in charge of its defense. The former Terrorist, a suave, devious exviscount, had once been an officer, but was more adept at conquests of the boudoir. He quickly delegated command to General Napoleon Buonaparte, who thought the king could have held the palace in 1792 if he had used his Swiss Guards and their cannon. Here was a man, Barras thought, who would show the Paris mobs no mercy.

VENDÉMIAIRE[6]   On October 5, 1795, the mobs marched on the Tuileries Palace, pikes high, red liberty caps bobbing, shouting the "Marseillaise." The scene was familiar. Paris was intimi-

---

[6] From the month of the Revolutionary calendar, adopted 1792, in force through 1805. Ordinary dates will be used in this book, or the corresponding supplied for revolutionary dates.

dating another government. Since the day of the Bastille, July 14, 1789, Paris had called the turn in the Revolution. The people marched confidently, sure of success, though Napoleon warned he would use artillery. He had emplaced cannon—40 of them seized from the unreliable National Guard the night before—to cover the approaches to the Tuileries. They were loaded with grapeshot, nails, scrap iron, and chains.

The people came on, flooding down the canyon-narrow streets that converged on the palace. Buonaparte gave no order. The cannoneers waited, growing nervous as the crowds came into view and the noise swelled. Soon the people were almost upon the guns, the front ranks hesitating, those behind pushing them forward. Fire! The cannon boomed, cutting bloody swaths into the mobs. The people fled, leaving the dead and dying, the dismembered bodies on the bloody pavement. Paris would never again, in that generation, dictate to the nation.

At 2 A.M. on October 6 Napoleon wrote his brother Joseph: "The enemy attacked us at the Tuileries. We killed a large number of them. . . . All is quiet. As usual, I haven't a scratch." General Buonaparte had done what no commander in Paris had had the stomach to do before—beginning with the Count de Launay, who might have held the Bastille if he had used all his weapons. He was promoted to major general, but many officers thought him a butcher, and the people hated him.

Nevertheless, by grace of Napoleon, the Convention's new government, the Directory, came into existence. Four years later he would replace it with his own. Meanwhile he would give France a taste of glory which would become an addiction.

JOSEPHINE   If the people cringed at the sight of Buonaparte, Paris society, where the women ruled, was dying to meet the shocking master-of-cannon. He got invitations to the salons, and at that of Madame Tallien, fell in love with Josephine de Beauharnais. She was dark-haired, brown-eyed, dainty of feature, willowy, and endowed perfectly for the gowns in high fashion, which revealed the bust—altogether or through diaphanous material.

Born in Martinique, she was the widow of the Viscount de

Beauharnais, guillotined during the Terror, and had barely escaped execution herself. She had been rescued by Jean-Lambert Tallien, another ex-Terrorist now serving the Directory, who had married Josephine's close friend, Thérésa Cabarrús.[7] Josephine was thirty-two, six years older than Napoleon, and the mother of two children—Eugène, fourteen, and Hortense, twelve.

Napoleon, who had had little experience with women, proposed marriage. Amused by his passion and his naïveté, Josephine became his mistress, then decided he might do for a husband. He would provide security for her family and probably be away often, leaving her to enjoy life. On March 9, 1796, they were married.

The Buonaparte family was shocked—not because of Josephine's age or other children, but because of her reputation. Was Napoleon blind? A denizen of the salons of Paris, she lived in luxury, but had no fortune. Her needs had been met by a succession of lovers, including Barras, now a director.[8] In addition to important "friends," she had "pets," such as the perfumed little Lieutenant Hippolyte Charles. The Buonapartes had to accept the marriage gracefully. But, since Josephine's life-style for years returned to "normal" when Napoleon departed, they were always hostile. Later, the Beauharnais children were seen as rivals.

BONAPARTE Almost simultaneous with his marriage, Napoleon was appointed commander of the Army of Italy, and departed after only a few days with his new wife. En route to Nice, his headquarters, he began signing his name Bonaparte. The name change coincided with the beginning of a rise to fame beyond even his own imagining.

In 1796, however, few would have predicted a brilliant future for General Bonaparte—even as a military man, much less a political leader. He was just another Johnny-come-lately

---

[7] Thérésa Tallien, divorced from the Marquis de Fontenay, was setting records for "naked" styles in Paris. Later as First Consul, Napoleon ordered her home to "put on some clothes."

[8] One of the five-man national executive council.

general. He had an army, but it was a motley array of ill-disciplined and ragged men barely able to guard the Italian border. Some said the command was Barras' reward for making Josephine an "honest woman." Napoleon's tender letters to Josephine give this the lie, but the story did him harm. Further, some thought that the directors meant to "bury" Bonaparte: the Army of Italy was expected to play no major part in the war.

Then too, much about Bonaparte offended his fellow officers. Most new generals were opportunists, but his case seemed flagrant. His battle experience against foreign enemies was almost nil. He was viewed by the battle-hardened veterans of war against Allied armies as a "staff man"—sure to fail as a commander.

He was considered a foreigner by many. He had a slight Italian accent; it was worse when he was angry. Most officers had some provincial accent—the Gascons, Alsatians, and others, but they were French of long standing. Napoleon's size also worked against him. He was, in fact, at about 5 feet 2, taller than most of the French recruits, who averaged 5 feet. But French officers and high officials—as in most countries in any era—were well above average height. His subordinates literally looked down on him.

Without a doubt, General Bonaparte took up his first major command with the cards stacked against him. But he saw only great opportunity ahead. Like the high-wire walker who strides confidently forward, he knew he would not fall.

CHAPTER TWO

Hero, Dictator, and Emperor

RESHAPING AN ARMY   General Bonaparte met his officers in mid-March 1796. At their head stood Generals André Masséna and Pierre Augereau—big, burly, hard-drinking ex-sergeants. As Napoleon approached, Masséna recalled, he looked like a boy riding his father's horse, but later, afoot—9 feet tall. Augereau admitted the "little bastard" scared him. They had been treated to the Napoleonic presence—the eagle-sharp stare of the blue-gray eyes, the coiled-spring air of suppressed violence that demanded attention.

Soon the officers also discovered that Napoleon knew more about the Army of Italy than they did. He had reviewed all available reports and plans. In later years he would advertise himself as the unbeatable man-of-destiny; the real secret of his success was preparation and hard work. He drove them to the wall with questions; he demanded that they discipline their men, round up deserters, and empty the hospitals of malingerers. Thereafter he harrassed them day and night. "I passed as an *homme terrible* . . . among the officers. . . ."

His approach to the men was different. He moved freely among them, tasting their food, looking over their uniforms, equipment, and arms. He learned their names, their records, and made promotions out of hand. With the help of Joseph, consul at Genoa, a neutral port, and Saliceti, supplier to the army, he got them better food, clothing, weapons, and prompter pay. It was not enough—but he promised the wealth of Italy— there for the taking. They decided "the little corporal" was a man to follow. "They had the instinct [to feel] . . . camaraderie. . . . They knew I was their patron."

Napoleon's accomplishment amounted to a miracle of leadership. In a month he marched, and what had been a disgruntled rabble proved itself a fighting force. He had breathed into it his own spirit and will to win. Lazare Carnot, now minister of war, was impressed; he sent reenforcements and more supplies.

In all that he did in later years Napoleon showed the same ability to influence men—in civil as well as military affairs. His presence, energy, ferocity alternated with charm, his posing, his facility with words, his intelligence and incredible memory for detail carried him through. Almost twenty years later, a prisoner aboard the British warship *Bellerophon*, he had captain and crew at his beck and call within days.

THE CAMPAIGN   The Directory's objective in 1796 was to defeat Austria—the only major opponent remaining on the Continent —though Austria had minor allies in Germany and Italy. Britain confined itself to the seas. Prussia and Spain had made peace in 1795. In 1794–95 the Netherlands had been overrun, Belgium— the Austrian Netherlands—annexed to France, and the United Provinces converted into the Batavian Republic.

Two large armies, under General Jean Baptiste Jourdan and General Jean Victor Moreau, were to drive on Vienna down the Danube. Napoleon's army, meanwhile, was to create a diversion in Italy, tie up Austrian troops there and discourage Austria's allies—the principal ones Piedmont-Sardinia, the Papal States, and Naples.

General Bonaparte upset the grand strategy by turning the Italian theater into the main one. The Army of Italy marched in mid-April. In five days Napoleon had won major battles that isolated the Piedmontese; the king, Victor Amadeus, asked for a truce. The other Italian states shortly followed suit. The Austrians withdrew into the Quadrilateral, four fortresses guarding the Alpine passes to Vienna. By midsummer they held only Mantua. Action centered on the siege of the fortress and repelling Austrian forces trying to relieve it. Napoleon repeatedly displayed personal courage which awed his troops, as at Arcola, where he seized a regimental standard and led the way across the Adige bridge. When Mantua finally fell in February 1797, Napoleon struck for Vienna. The Austrians' best commander, the Archduke Charles, tried to stop him, but could not. When Napoleon reached Leoben, 100 miles from Vienna, Charles called for a truce (April 1797). The war was over. Peace was made in October 1797 at Campo Formio.

KING OF MOMBELLO   General Bonaparte meanwhile returned to Mombello (Montebello, in Piedmont), where he received in royal style and arranged settlements with scant attention to the Directory. In September his general, Augereau, supported a *coup* which replaced two directors and purged the councils. Napoleon expressed contempt for the government: "Do you think I have conquered for the benefit of the lawyers? What an idea!" He oversaw the conversion of Genoa into the Ligurian Republic and completed the formation, begun in 1796, of the Cisalpine Republic, comprising former Austrian duchies, some papal territory,[1] and part of Venetia which he took even though that state was friendly. He levied indemnities at will, and finally decided the terms of peace with Austria.

At Campo Formio (October 1797) he gave to Austria Venice and its Istrian and Dalmation possessions, but retained the

---

[1] Milan, Modena, Mantua; Bologna and Ferrara.

Ionian Islands off Greece—stepping-stones to the East. The Austrian emperor formally ceded Belgium to France and, as Holy Roman Emperor, the west bank of the Rhine as well. He agreed to a conference at Rastadt to rearrange the map of Germany and recognized France's "sister republics." Napoleon had made the *Grande Nation* dominant on the Continent, encroaching on previously Austrian preserves in Germany and Italy. Austria was sure to fight back when it recovered its strength. The thought did not bother Napoleon; he helped lay plans (effected in 1798) for Roman and Swiss Republics.[2] This further extension of French power, accompanied in Rome by the imprisonment of the pope, did nothing to calm the Holy Roman Emperor.

THE CISALPINE REPUBLIC Napoleon's work in the Cisalpine Republic prefigured his later policies and operating methods outside France. The constitution of the republic was drawn up by "sure" Italian liberals—Francesco Melzi, Ferdinando Marescalchi, and others—and not submitted to the voters. It was more democratic, however, than the current French Constitution of the Year III. It provided for universal manhood suffrage and a single-chamber legislature. The voters, however, elected delegates, who had to meet property qualifications, through a system of electors. Moreover, certification of legislators was by a *consulta* of state, an elite council, initially appointed by Napoleon.[3]

The constitution, nevertheless, was radical and constructive. It abolished feudalism, including church privileges, guilds, and entail. It included a bill of rights guaranteeing equality before the law, in taxation, and of opportunity, and freedom of religion. It prepared northern Italy for future Napoleonic governments, where equality, opportunity, and progress would be emphasized, but political liberty and the popular voice suppressed.

[2] Naples was converted into the Parthenopean Republic in 1799, giving the French temporary domination of the Italian Peninsula.
[3] The Directory eliminated universal manhood suffrage in Italy in 1798; Napoleon restored it in 1800.

EGYPT At the end of 1797 Napoleon returned in triumph to Paris; crowds followed his carriage everywhere. "Vive Bonaparte! Vive la République!" The directors, though frightened at his popularity, aped the people's adoration. There were parades, fireworks displays, receptions, dinners, dances, and command theater performances. The Institut de France (see p. 50) elected General Bonaparte a member. "The greatest conquests," he told the intellectuals, "are those made against ignorance." He was modest, dignified, affable—but publicly criticized the constitution. Privately, Napoleon told Joseph that he meant to destroy the corrupt Directory when the time was right. "Our dreams of a republic were illusions of youth."

Until the time was right, he determined to keep his reputation alive: that meant action. The only enemy of France still fighting was Great Britain. How could he strike at *les Anglais?* The directors offered him command of an army forming at Boulogne to invade England. He refused it. He and Talleyrand, now foreign minister, had another plan.

Talleyrand presented it to the Institut: Seize Egypt, destroy British influence in the Ottoman empire, cut its trade routes to India, encourage Indian rebels, perhaps invade India. Egypt, nominally a vassal state of Turkey, was ruled by the Mamelukes. Talleyrand was to convince the sultan that France would restore Ottoman power in Egypt. Napoleon asked to command the expedition.

The Directory agreed; it was pleased to rid itself of Bonaparte and "invest" a small army—35,000 men. Britain was having economic difficulties; revolution was brewing in Ireland, with Protestants and Catholics united; Tippoo Sahib, sultan of Mysore, was making trouble in India, and was in contact with the French. If Bonaparte had even limited success, the enemy might bid for peace. If he failed—no great loss.

On May 19, 1798, Napoleon's expedition sailed from Toulon, seized Malta in June, and on July 1 landed in Egypt. Only four days before the landing, Admiral Horatio Nelson had been lying in wait off Egypt with the British Mediterranean fleet, but had left to resupply in Sicily. He returned on August 1 to blow the French fleet out of the water. He trapped the French army in Egypt, but could not prevent the conquest.

On July 21, in a single great battle, fought before Cairo, in the shadow of the Pyramids—"Soldiers, forty centuries look down upon you."—Napoleon assured his mastery of the country. The Mameluke cavalry, brave to the point of insanity, but with medieval weapons, charged again and again, only to be slaughtered by artillery and musket fire. This ruling caste had originally been the Caliph's elite guard of slave-troops, taken as boys in Europe—largely in the Balkans—and reared as Moslems, and still "recruited" in Europe. Napoleon admired their courage and was fascinated by their costumes—silken jackets, billowing pantaloons, turbans. He recruited some of them, who later gave an exotic touch to the Imperial Guard. The best known was his giant personal guard, Roustan, always near his master, curved scimitar at the ready.

Napoleon established a government and put to work a coterie of scientists, other scholars, and artists, whose work gave Egyptians a lasting respect for French culture. Napoleon's reforms made less of an impression, though he worked at everything from education to land tenure.

In 1798 Turkey declared war on France, allying with Britain and Russia. In February 1799 Napoleon struck into Syria,[4] but was stopped at Acre (Akko, near Haifa). Unable to take the fortress, his troops dying of disease, hunger, and thirst, he learned that the British were transporting a Turkish army to Egypt. He retreated (May 1799).

ABOUKIR   On July 25, 1799 Napoleon, with 7000 troops, met a Turkish force of 20,000 on the beach at Aboukir. His artillery shattered their ranks; his infantry columns drove in. Behind them came the cavalry of the Gascon Joachim Murat, driving the enemy into the surf, charging, cutting, trampling until the waves frothed with blood. The awed British admiral, Sir Sidney Smith, watching from his flagship, quickly agreed to take the pitiful survivors away.

[4] Napoleon did not invade modern Syria, but what is now Israel, via the Gaza Strip.

RETURN TO FRANCE   Bonaparte had again covered himself with glory. But France was again at war in Europe, and doing badly. Opportunity lay there. Without orders, Napoleon set sail in a small ship with Murat and a few others, by a minor miracle eluded the British fleet, and in October was in France.

The news of his victory at Aboukir had just arrived. He rode to Paris through villages full of cheering people who saw him as a savior. The Directory, which had issued orders, which Napoleon did not receive, to return with his army, bowed to his popularity and gave him a hero's welcome. His failures and abandonment of his army were ignored. Napoleon felt no guilt. He had returned to "save" France—to take over the government and win the war. Then he would worry about the army in Egypt. In 1802 he did repatriate the survivors who were then prisoners of the British.

THE SECOND COALITION   Britain, Russia, and Turkey had been joined in the Second Coalition by Sardinia-Piedmont, Austria, and lesser German states. During the spring and summer of 1799 the French were driven out of Italy, save Genoa, which was under siege. The Archduke Charles threatened the Rhine frontier. Russian armies in Switzerland had put Masséna on the defensive. An Anglo-Russian army under the duke of York had invaded the Netherlands. When Napoleon left Egypt France seemed headed for defeat, but by the time his reception was over in Paris, things were different. Austrian armies still challenged on the Rhine and at Genoa, but the Russians had been beaten in Switzerland. More important, Tsar Paul, convinced that Austria cared about nothing but recovering its own power, especially in northern Italy, ordered his troops home. The duke of York, defeated, evacuated the Netherlands.

Nevertheless, French morale was low.

THE DIRECTORY   The Directory had proved itself unstable; that is, it had never abided by its own constitution. Instead the Directory and councils were changed by *coups d'état.* There had been three major ones. No government, therefore, could be sure of its life span; the result was weakness and lack of public confidence. The last *coup,* in June 1799, had left the Directory in precarious balance. There were two Jacobins, Gohier and Moulin, two moderates, the Abbé Sieyès and Pierre Roger Ducos, and holding the balance, the durable Paul Barras. In the fall of 1799, therefore, anything was possible.

Belatedly, the government had coped well with the wars. Domestically, it had a better record than any revolutionary government before it. Its economic policies, for example, were the same, in essence, which Napoleon would follow. None of this, however, is relevant.

The people had lost faith in the Directory. This showed in various ways. In the chronically royalist Vendée and in Brittany, guerrillas were again out in force. Banditry was rife, travel very dangerous. Government securities and paper money were dropping in value. People had begun hoarding hard money, accelerating inflation. The Directory seemed paralyzed. Its opposition exaggerated its ills.

THE REVISIONISTS   The leader of the "constitutional revisionists" was a director, the Abbé Sieyès, author of the famous "What is the Third Estate?" active in politics since 1789. "I survived," he said of his role in the Convention during the Terror. Fearful of another Terror, he wanted a stronger executive and docile legislative bodies, selected, however, very indirectly, by universal manhood suffrage, to assure "confidence from below." His party really wanted a new government, not "revision." It included another director, Ducos; the foreign minister, Talleyrand; the minister of police, Joseph Fouché; and Napoleon's brothers Joseph and Lucien, the latter president of the Council of Five Hundred, the lower house of parliament. Joseph, a social lion, novelist, and *philosophe,* was friendly with the intelligentsia—Madame de Staël, Benjamin Constant, Chateaubriand, and others.[5] Joseph also drew scientists, artists, generals, and politicians to his soirées at Mortefontaine, near Paris. He won many over to the revisionists and persuaded others to remain neutral.

Although some revisionists, including Joseph, hoped for peaceful change, most knew that a *coup,* involving at least the threat of force, would be necessary. For months, Sieyès had been

[5] See pp. 39, 40, and 52 for identification.

looking for a "sword." He finally settled on Napoleon, though even Lucien Bonaparte warned that he would be hard to control. Sieyès wanted "his" general to become "Grand Elector," leaving real power to two civilian consuls.

BRUMAIRE On arrival in Paris, Napoleon immediately contacted the revisionists. The overthrow of the Directory was planned for 18–19 Brumaire (November 9–10, 1799).

On 18 Brumaire Sieyès and Ducos resigned their directorships, as did Barras, cowed by Talleyrand—another "man of 1789," a lame, wily, ex-bishop with the inscrutible face of a tabbycat. The other directors—Gohier and Moulin—were put under house arrest. The Council of Elders, the upper house of parliament, was summoned and told that a Jacobin plot was afoot—a new Terror imminent. Prompted, the Elders voted that the councils, elders and five hundred, meet the next day at the St.-Cloud palace—in the suburbs safe from the crowd—to consider this threat. For additional security they appointed General Bonaparte commander of troops in Paris, though most of the delegates knew there was no Jacobin plot.

Napoleon's assignment was opposed by Bernadotte, the Jacobin (i.e., loyal republican)[6] minister of war, who could have caused trouble. "Belle-Jambe" was an ex-sergeant popular with the rank and file. But his wife, Désirée Clary, and brother-in-law Joseph Bonaparte persuaded him not to interfere.

On 19 Brumaire the councils met amid much confusion. It was noon before the halls were ready; the palace was frigid. Troops massed in the gardens. Tempers were short. Napoleon went first before the Elders to demand revision of the constitution. With some grumbling, the body acquiesced. In the Council of Five Hundred the story was different. Lucien, president of the Council, could not keep order. Napoleon was greeted with anger. "Death to the traitor!" "Outlaw him!" Deputies pushed toward the front of the room. Caught in a crush, Napoleon either fainted or was knocked unconscious. He was carried from the room.

Lucien tried to restore order, and failing, rushed outside.

[6] After 1794, few of those called Jacobins were real Terrorists.

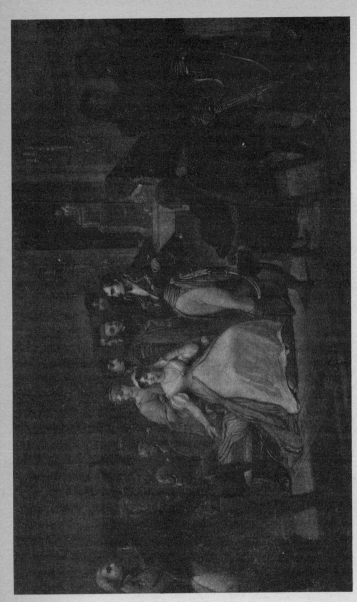

The morning of the 18th Brumaire (November 9, 1799). A group of the "constitutional revisionists" awaits implementation of the plot that will make Napoleon First Consul of France. Among those shown are, in the center, Josephine and Napoleon; behind them, Lucien Bonaparte, left, and Murat; in the right foreground, Cambacérès, seated, with Talleyrand. (*The New York Public Library*)

Napoleon was trying to rally the troops, but was still groggy and incoherent. Leaping on a horse, Lucien shouted that the palace was full of "assassins" and enemies of the people who must be driven out. Waving a sword, he promised to plunge it into Napoleon's heart if he betrayed the Republic. The troops cleared the halls at bayonet point. The deputies ran, tripping over their togalike robes of office and clutching their plumed hats, through the gardens and into the woods and fields. Lucien had saved the day, but, he later said, only because, at the time, it was "do or die."

The *coup* had succeeded, but not as the leaders desired. Most wanted the government changed with some semblance of legality. They reconvened the chambers, insofar as possible. In the early evening a rump of the councils voted executive power to a temporary consulate—Napoleon, Sieyès, and Ducos. Their responsibility was to produce a new constitution.

All this was still very irregular, but France was unmoved. T. S. Eliot once wrote: "Human kind cannot stand too much of reality. . . ." After ten years of revolution, unstable government, violence, and war, the people were numb. They were ready for a strong man who would tell them lies they wanted to hear—one who would discipline society and "preserve the Revolution."

NEW CONSTITUTION "Constitutions," said Napoleon, "should be short and obscure." That of the Year VIII was both. The government? "There is Bonaparte," said a Parisian. Sieyès' plan for universal manhood suffrage was adopted, but he himself was relegated to the Senate. The voters approved "Bonaparte"— 3,000,000 to 1500.

As First Consul, Napoleon had full executive power. He appointed his "co-rulers," the Second and Third Consuls, Jean Cambacérès and Charles François Lebrun, who were only advisers. The legal expert, Cambacérès, was an ex-Terrorist; Lebrun was a former bureaucrat of the Old Regime. These two made a balanced team for a government-of-all-talents. Also, Cambacérès was a huge, fat gourmet; Lebrun, trim and austere. The consuls named a majority of the Senate; their appointees selected the rest (total 60, later more). The Senate then named

Napoleon as First Consul. *(The New York Public Library)*

the members of the Tribunate (100) and the Corps Législatif (300); the former discussed legislation, the latter voted on it. Bills were drafted by a Council of State, appointed by the First Consul. To it were attached young "auditors," who did "leg work" and prepared for higher positions. The First Consul named ministers, military officers, and, directly or indirectly, all administrators, judges, and police officers.

All men over twenty-one could vote, except felons, prisoners, and the insane, but chose no representatives directly. France was divided into departments, and these into districts, cantons—for voting only—and municipalities. In each district the voters chose one-tenth of their number as electors, who chose one-tenth of themselves for the departmental list, which then selected one-tenth for the national list. From this list the Senate appointed deputies to the Tribunate and Corps Législatif. Only one man in 1000 had even a chance at national office.

To WAR AGAIN   His government was established, but France was still at war. Napoleon again took up the sword. Again Austria, as in 1796, was the only major enemy remaining, save Britain. He sent General Jean Moreau against the Austrians in Germany, while Masséna held the enemy at bay at Genoa. In May 1800 the First Consul himself, riding a mule, led a reserve army of 40,000 from Dijon through the snow-choked passes of the Alps and captured Milan. He was behind the Austrian army of General Melas. The enemy commander recovered more quickly, however, than Napoleon expected. At Marengo, on June 14, the armies met suddenly, and what began as a skirmish grew into an all-out bloodletting. Napoleon, his troops dispersed, was hard pressed, but reinforcements arrived under General Louis Desaix, who marched to the sound of the guns. Italy was won. It was a great victory, though Desaix, the hero of the day, was killed. In December, Moreau triumphed in Germany, at the battle of Hohenlinden, and threatened Vienna. Austria surrendered.

PEACE ON THE CONTINENT   The Austrian Holy Roman Emperor made peace at Lunéville, in Lorraine, on February 9, 1801. French possession of Belgium and the west bank of the Rhine was confirmed. A reorganization of Germany was agreed upon, which would drastically reduce the number of small states, the main support of the emperor. Larger ones like Bavaria had the strength for independent action; these Napoleon intended to make allies. France's "sister republics" were recognized, except those in Rome and Naples, which Napoleon chose not to restore.

The pope was allowed his possessions in consideration of concluding a Concordat with France (see pp. 31, 41, 42). Naples had been reconquered by its Bourbon monarchs with heavy, if temporary, popular support. They agreed to admit French garrisons; reconquest seemed unprofitable—for the moment.

PEACE WITH BRITAIN   Britain, its continental allies beaten, was further shaken when Russia suspended trade, and Paul I, temporarily, got all the Baltic powers to do likewise. The great war minister William Pitt resigned, which allowed Henry Addington, his successor, to sue for peace with France.

The negotiators met at Amiens—Lord Cornwallis for Britain, Joseph Bonaparte for France. Cornwallis was probably the most respected public figure, save Pitt, in Britain. Yorktown, which Americans remembered, had been unusual in a distinguished career including the offices of Governor General of India and Viceroy of Ireland. At sixty-seven, tall, soldierly, full of dignity, he exemplified *milord Anglais* to the French, who were honored by his coming. He refused to negotiate with "that scoundrel" Talleyrand. Joseph proved the perfect substitute; they became fast friends, and completed their work in record time.

Cornwallis, perhaps, forgot that he was really negotiating with Napoleon. The treaty of Amiens (signed March 27, 1802) contained no commercial agreement. There was only the promise of one, which was not to be honored. The British agreed to restore all conquests except Ceylon (formerly Dutch), and Trinidad (Spanish), and to evacuate Malta and Elba. The French agreed not to garrison troops in Naples and to respect the integrity of Portugal and Holland. This meant to the British, among other things, that the ports of these countries would be open to them. They found that Napoleon had another view.

THE CONCORDAT OF 1801   The Concordat of 1801 with Pope Pius VII rounded out Napoleon's peacemaking. It was an international treaty but also the key to ending the royalist-clerical rebellion in the Vendée and Brittany, in progress since 1793, and reunite the Catholic clergy, split since 1791 when part refused to take an oath to the government. Negotiations began after Marengo, facilitated by the restoration of the Papal States.[7] With the beginning of talks, most of the rebel leaders in France accepted the amnesty offered by Napoleon. He appointed one ex-rebel, the Abbé Bernier, chief French negotiator for the Concordat, with Joseph Bonaparte. The First Consul "encouraged" more rebels to take amnesty by hounding them mercilessly and executing captives. The rebellion was soon dead.

The royalists hoped that since General Bonaparte was wooing the pope, he might return Louis XVIII, the Bourbon pretender, to the throne. Louis wrote "his" general. No, replied Napoleon—the bodies of 300,000 Frenchmen barred the way. Napoleon knew that the rebellion had been by peasants motivated principally by religion, not royalism. For the sake of his power, he made terms with the pope; he did not need the king. (The terms and implementation of the Concordat are covered in Chapter 3.)

General Bonaparte brought full peace to Europe for the first time in ten years. For good measure he ended an undeclared "corsair war" with the United States (see pp. 151–152). Although the treaty with Britain collapsed in little more than a year, France enjoyed a respite of almost five years (1800–1805) from war on the Continent. During this time Napoleon's government(s) gave the nation enormous benefits, and began or completed projects which are still affecting French life. These will be the subject of Chapter 3.

CONSOLIDATION OF POWER   Reform and conciliation among all Frenchmen were the themes of the Consulate. At the same time, Napoleon tightened his authority and eliminated his opposition.

The first minister he appointed was Joseph Fouché,

[7] Except those in the Cisalpine Republic.

minister of police. Ex-cleric and teacher, polished, aristocratic in appearance, he was nevertheless an ex-Terrorist directly responsible for the death of hundreds. He had turned on Robespierre in time, however, and as Minister of Police of the Directory helped bring Napoleon to power. The First Consul knew that Fouché had to be watched, but he was a talented man, a policeman by instinct. Napoleon needed him; he used him.[8]

The restoration of law and order was much aided by the Concordat. In addition, the police were reenforced, and at times backed by the army. Highways were made safe for travel; robber bands were destroyed; city streets patrolled more efficiently. Vagrants were relegated to prisons or workhouses. All this was much applauded. But Napoleon's forces of order were also used for repression.

Fouché's first big case was the "infernal machine" plot, an attempt to bomb Napoleon's carriage as he drove to the Opera on Christmas Eve, 1800. A number of bystanders were killed, but not the First Consul. Within hours Fouché had identified the culprits; they were royalists. Napoleon, however, wanted to move against the "Jacobins," who were trying to strengthen the legislative bodies. He denounced them by *senatus consultum* (decree with the consent of the Senate). For the "protection of the constitution," special tribunals sent some 120 to the Seychelles Islands, in the Indian Ocean; over 700 others were imprisoned. Three months later, Napoleon resurrected Fouché's evidence and accused the royalists. Many were imprisoned; two were shot.

In the spring of 1802 Napoleon purged the legislative bodies. One-fifth of the deputies, chosen by lot, were supposed to retire. The Senate picked their replacements from the national list, which was proper, but also chose those to retire — Napoleon's enemies — which was unconstitutional.

Fouché had already begun the censorship of newspapers, magazines, journals, theatrical productions, and even private correspondence. Ultimately only four political papers were

[8] Until 1810, when he caught him dealing with the British. Even then he found other work for the then Duke d'Otrante.

allowed in Paris: the *Moniteur, Journal de Paris, Journal de l'Empire* and *Gazette de France.* There was one for each department. Napoleon also "reformed" the Institut de France, eliminating intellectual "troublemakers." (See p. 40).

In 1802 Napoleon asked the Senate to proclaim him Consul for life. The Senate, in a rare moment of courage, refused; the Council of State made the proclamation. A plebiscite confirmed the life consulship—3,600,000 to 8600—and amendments to the constitution.[9] The latter authorized Napoleon to appoint 40 additional senators, and to call and dismiss the legislative assemblies at will. Electoral colleges, comprising only the richest citizens—though voting continued as usual—replaced departmental lists. Moreover, the Tribunate was reduced to 50 and divided into sections, each to discuss one kind of legislation only. The effectiveness of the only semipopular vocal house was all but destroyed. It was dismissed permanently in 1807. As before, the Corps Législatif voted without debating.

THE DUKE D'ENGHIEN   In 1803–04 Napoleon and Fouché made a final end to serious Bourbon opposition. Royalists in London were hoping to assassinate or kidnap the First Consul, then return Louis XVIII to the throne backed by an army of French exiles from Germany. Fouché's agents infiltrated the group, encouraged them, and lured the leaders Georges Cadoudal and General Charles Pichegru to Paris. They called on General Moreau, named to them, falsely, as a sympathizer. All three were arrested. Cadoudal was executed. Pichegru died mysteriously in prison. Moreau was exiled from France, thus eliminating a national hero and rival of Napoleon.

It remained to find the Bourbon prince who was supposed to lead the army from Germany. Fouché's agents fixed on the Duc d'Enghien, exiled in Baden. He had no army, but he was a Bourbon, the heir of the Condés, first princes of the blood, and he was nearby. Napoleon's soldiers crossed into Germany, illegally, and brought him to Vincennes on March 20, 1804. He was shot at dawn the next morning.

[9] Now termed the Constitution of the Year X.

Napoleon did not apologize. It was necessary, he said, for the safety of France. He repeated this in his will.[10]

It was an act of terror. "Bonaparte has joined the Convention," said Fouché, laughingly. It was a throwing down of the gauntlet to the exiled Bourbons and European monarchs in general. Napoleon was planning to become emperor, and defying them to interfere. In addition he wanted to impress upon the French that his life was in perpetual danger, that his government depended on that life, and that this would not be so if a hereditary monarchy were created.

The initial reaction of the French, even the hardened Parisians, was adverse. The Condés had produced famous soldiers for generations; the duke was young, handsome, and the last of his line. But they soon saw Napoleon's point. A shock went through the courts of Europe, but they reacted in fear as well as horror.

THE EMPIRE Napoleon's life-style had long since changed. In late 1802, wrote Miot de Melito: "The Tuileries and Saint-Cloud were no longer the residences of the chief magistrate of a republic, but the court of a sovereign." The same year Napoleon founded the Legion of Honor, which conferred a decoration, rank, and pensions to its members.[11] Republicans accused him of creating a new nobility. He argued that merit was being rewarded, nothing more.

The Empire was proclaimed in May 1804 by *senatus consultum* and approved by plebiscite. By the Constitution of the Year XII, Napoleon was made Emperor of the French; the crown was to descend to the male heirs, if any, of Napoleon, then Joseph, then Louis. The emperor was also given the right to adopt an heir, a thing unprecedented since Roman times. He could also appoint senators without limit.

The coronation was staged in Notre Dame on December

---

[10] Although he had previously blamed Talleyrand.

[11] The medal was suspended from a blood-red ribbon (cut from revolutionary liberty caps, said English propaganda); rank was from "Grand Cross" to Chevalier (Knight). It was awarded both to military men and civilians, who received from 5000 to 250 francs a year. The Legion persists in France today.

2, 1804. Pope Pius VII occupied a seat of honor, thus seemingly
blessing the emperor's accession; but, forewarned, he did not
crown him. Napoleon crowned himself, his hand on his sword,
symbolizing that he owed none of his powers to the church but
was monarch " . . . by the unanimous will of the French people
and the army." Moreover, he used the regalia and sword of
Charlemagne, brought from Aix-la-Chapelle (Aachen), empha-
sizing that he was not the successor of the Bourbons but of the
great King of the Franks. The only concrete concession to the
pope was the agreement that the Revolutionary calendar would
be abolished in favor of the Christian (Gregorian) as of January
1, 1806.

WAR CLOUDS Napoleon's relations with the Vatican would
worsen apace. Moreover his assumption of the imperial dignity
had been a direct affront to the Austrian Holy Roman Emperor,
by tradition the successor of Charlemagne. As First Consul, his
aggressive behavior had alarmed not only Austrian but other
European powers as well. Britain had already, in 1803, resumed
hostilities with France. In 1805 Britain would gain allies on the
Continent and general war would begin anew.

Before discussing these events, however, we shall devote
a chapter to Napoleon's performance as civil executive in France.

CHAPTER THREE

Napoleonic France

*We have finished the romance of the Revolution;
history must now begin.*
— Napoleon to the
Council of State (1800)

BRUTE FORCE solidified Napoleon's authority. But
the real source of his power was his immense popularity with the mass of the French people. It
stemmed, in part, from the glory he brought France.
But the pride he excited in them was mixed with
trust and gratitude because he gave them perhaps
the best government France had ever had. In the
process he reformed the nation's institutions so
thoroughly that his influence is evident even today.

Napoleon was an incomparable civil executive. His domestic accomplishments certify to that;
his work outside France (covered in later chapters)
compounds the evidence. It is not merely because
he was a superb soldier, but an organizer, administrator, and lawgiver that he deserves the appella-
tion "great."

THE NAPOLEONIC METHOD   *"Organiser* is a word of the Empire," wrote Balzac. Napoleon loved efficiency. Nothing that flawed it was allowable—within practical limits. He was also still a Rousseauist, determined to govern for the people—not by their will, except as expressed in plebiscites granting very broad mandates. His approach was in line with the will of the French people expressed in the *cahiers* of 1789. They had not called for destruction of the monarchy, but for more efficient government, speedier justice, equality in taxation, and the elimination of privileges. He reduced liberty in France, but with the idea of introducing more equality—in the legal sense, and in terms of opportunity.

His operating method was well demonstrated by the way he pushed through the Constitution of the Year VIII (pp. 27, 29). In February 1800, after two months of bombardment by propaganda in favor of the document, the people were asked to vote. They approved overwhelmingly. But the constitution had already been in effect since December 1799. The Senate and the legislative bodies had already been appointed.

SOCIETY   As First Consul one of Napoleon's earliest acts was to invite back the *émigrés* and exiles—royalist and republican alike—with a few exceptions, including the royal family and its most fanatic supporters.

Why shouldn't the exiles return? Napoleon asked. "Where is the revolutionary who would not have faith in the order of things when Fouché is minister [of police]? What gentleman, if he is French, cannot make a life where a Périgord [Talleyrand, of the high aristocracy] will have power."[1] Careers were open to nobles, ex-terrorists, exiles of all revolutionary governments. Lazare Carnot came back to serve briefly as minister of war, then

---

[1] Joseph Bonaparte, *Mémoires et correspondance du roi Joseph,* 10 vols. Edited by A. du Casse, 2d ed. (Paris: 1854), I, pp. 81–82. Quotation in slightly different form in Louis Villat, *La Révolution française et l'empire,* Vol. II: *Napoléon* (Paris, 1947), p. 6. See also *Correspondance de Napoléon Ier,* 32 vols. (Paris, 1858–1869), Items 4398, 4439, 4457, 4467, 4468, 4630, 4997, 5634, 5874, 6050, and passim; and Miot de Melito, *Mémoires,* 3 vols. 3d ed. (Paris, 1880), I, p. 265.

in the Tribunate. The Marquis de Lafayette was one of the first to return.[2] He graced the salons of the Bonapartes for a few years and served them indirectly, notably in their dealings with Americans. But he was allowed no real political role—until 1815—and then it was a mistake. Most nobles employed by Napoleon were those who had not emigrated, or like Talleyrand, had left France but briefly. Typical were the Counts de Ségur. The father, Louis Philippe, became a senator; his son, Philippe Paul de Ségur, became Napoleon's aide-de-camp and a general. The latter authored a famous account of the Russian campaign. Aristocrats were denied their ancient privileges, but regained much property and used their titles socially.

It was the middle class, the bourgeoisie, however, which benefited most from Napoleon's policy of "careers open to talent" as well as his economic programs (see p. 42ff). Talent was the key word, but talent without education was difficult to display, except in the military, and some was required even there. Members of the bourgeoisie, with fewer numbers of minor nobility, populated the ministry, the Council of State, the bureaucracy, and the judiciary. Outside officialdom, the middle class expanded greatly with the growth of industry. Even in landholding, their possessions vastly outweighed those of the nobility—old and new—in 1815. Peasant holdings also increased to upward of 60 percent of all land, mostly in small parcels, but a "rural middle class," with larger holdings, also formed. It was the sons of the middle class—old and new—who had the easiest access to the schools (see p. 49ff), and thus opportunity to perpetuate their status. In the army, every private was given to believe that he "carried a marshal's baton in his knapsack." Joachim Murat, son of Gascon peasants, became a marshal, as did Pierre Augereau and André Masséna, who were of equally low origins. But most of the marshals were of the middle class, like Jean Baptiste Jourdan, son of a surgeon, or of the minor nobility, like Louis Davout.

[2] He had fled after the fall of Louis XVI (1792), only to be imprisoned as a revolutionary by Austria. Freed at Napoleon's request in 1797, he had still been banned from France.

Napoleon's new nobility came from the elite of government and the army. The marshals and generals in particular were encouraged to find wives among the old nobility—and many did. "In ten years the nobility will all be one," Napoleon said. To some degree it was so. His own family, all given princely (four later royal) rank, intermarried with European royalty, and their children continued to do so after his death. Lucien, however, got his princedom from the pope.

Still it was the middle class and the new nobility who were the progressive element when the Empire fell. After a short-lived triumph of the old aristocracy, it was they who dominated the governments of the nineteenth century. While Napoleon ruled, however, there was an astonishing harmony in society.

Even the intellectuals, temporarily, were propitiated. Napoleon, however, soon clashed with Madame de Staël, part feminist, part aging coquette, all ego. Enamored of the First Consul, she tried to impress him at every opportunity—and was rebuffed repeatedly. "Who was the greatest woman of history?" she once asked. "The one who had the most children," he growled.[3] But temporarily the First Consul kept on good terms with Benjamin Constant, who was in the Institut and, briefly, in the Tribunate, and induced Chateaubriand to accept a diplomatic post. Joseph Bonaparte, cospirit of all three, was considered by British intelligence to be the most influential man in France—until 1803.

By that time legal opposition to the regime had become impossible. As early as January 1800 Fouché suppressed 60 of the 73 newspapers in Paris. The work continued apace. (See pp. 32–33.) Napoleon railed against the "speculative and hypothetical" in politics and blamed irresponsible intellectuals for

---

[3] Anecdote attributed to General Gourgaud. Quoted in F. G. Healey, *The Literary Culture of Napoleon* (Geneva, 1959), p. 139, footnote. Madame Germaine de Staël (1766–1817), daughter of the Swiss banker Jacques Necker, sometime minister of finance of Louis XVI, married the Swedish Baron de Staël. She was famous for her novels *(Corinne; Delphine)* and literary and political tracts—and for her numerous love affairs. In her *Considerations sur la révolution française* (1818) and *Dix années de'exil* (1821), published after her death, she took revenge on Napoleon.

confusing the people, creating factions, and inviting the "anarchy" common under former governments. He would not have it. "I respect public opinion . . . but it is capricious. . . . It is for the government and those who support it to enlighten it. . . ." He called for private debate but public harmony on political matters.[4] This was an instruction difficult to accept.

"Troublemakers" multiplied, particularly in the Institut. Napoleon responded by "reorganizing" the body. The sections for the science and art were left intact, but that of "moral and political sciences" was dissolved, and two bodies appointed to replace it — French language and literature, and history and literature. The *Idéologues,* including Benjamin Constant, who had dominated the old section, were not reappointed. Constant objected too vociferously and was exiled from France. Madame de Staël followed. Chateaubriand resigned his official position and went into provincial exile.[5]

Harmony of opinion was achieved at the sacrifice of freedom of expression. In view of the benefits afforded by the new government, however, there was little objection. Much of it came from within the Bonaparte family — from Joseph and Lucien. Few mourned the exit of the chattering Madame de Staël. Intellectual life did not stagnate (see p. 52ff). Moreover the exiles were not hounded once they had left France. They traveled freely, even in the satellites, and their writings were published abroad.

It is often ignored that except for a brief period early in the Revolution censorship had always been practiced in France, and that every government since Napoleon's time has used it, including that in power today. His system, therefore, was no novelty.

[4] *Correspondance de Napoléon,* 6591. "Exposé de la situation de la République" (February 20, 1803). Miot, *Mémoires,* I, 323. Napoléon, *Pensées pour l'action.* Edited by E. Driault (Paris, 1943), pp. 30, 31. Hereinafter cited as Napoléon, *Pensées.*

[5] The *Idéologues* were liberals who fought for active legislative bodies and freedom of the press. Benjamin Constant de Rebecque (1787–1830) had already been purged from the Tribunate for his "disruptive" oratory. A political theorist and journalist, he was much influenced by Madame de Staël. On Chateaubriand, see p. 52.

The clergy fell into line, devising a new catechism to teach loyalty to the regime. Napoleon was diplomatic in his management of them; privately he was cynical. "My second gendarmerie," he called them. Religion, he said, was "a mystery of the social order"—a means of controlling the populace. The Concordat had been negotiated to give him a disciplined hierarchy to inculcate proper attitudes in the people—as it had for the old kings. "One does not govern men who do not believe in God," he said; "one shoots them."

RELIGIOUS POLICY The Concordat recognized Roman Catholicism as "the religion of the majority of Frenchmen." The French government would nominate the clergy; the pope would invest the bishops, and could reject nominees. The government agreed to pay the clergy; the pope, in effect, gave up claim to church property confiscated during the Revolution.

As Napoleon had expected, the church resumed what approximated its traditional place in society. This was especially important to the peasants, who were conservative and religious, and comprised more than 80 percent of the population. Titles to church property were guaranteed. This increased Napoleon's popularity and power also because it attached to him all those who had acquired such property. Not least important, again, were the peasants. Though their holdings were in small parcels, they still owned 50 percent of the former church lands, and would get more.

The Catholic church was no longer established—the sole official one. Religious freedom, plus laws allowing civil marriage and divorce, won over most anticlericals. Men could leave property to legitimate heirs not "certified" by religious marriage. Pius VII accepted all this, but he objected violently to the Organic Articles, by which Napoleon provided "against the more serious inconveniences of a literal execution of the Concordat." Thereby the church could perform its functions only in compliance with police regulations. Authority to set doctrine was given to the French bishops, and thus denied to the pope. This was in line with Gallican tradition, as Napoleon knew, and strengthened his hand in France. Finally, regulations were provided for Protestant churches also, and pay granted their ministers.

Nothing was said about Jews, but by later legislation Napoleon took them under government protection and sponsored their integration into French society. Their money-lending activities were regulated, which inconvenienced some but also shielded them from charges of usury. Meetings of Jewish leaders with officials were called at intervals to discuss their problems. And of course their right to worship was insured.

Napoleon's religious policies guided later governments. The Concordat, despite the emperor's imprisonment of the pope (1809) and confiscation of his lands, remained on the books. It was the working agreement between France and the Vatican until 1905.

FISCAL AND ECONOMIC MATTERS   The most basic reforms were fiscal and economic. Faith in the government's credit had to be insured and economic growth and full employment fostered before other work could go forward.

In January 1800 Napoleon created the Bank of France, modeled after the Bank of England, with the stock owned partly by the government, part privately. It handled the government's money, issued its securities, and also did private business. One of its functions was to keep the economy stable by supplying funds to enterprisers at whatever rate seemed required by the circumstances. Loans at 2 percent, for example, were available during the crisis of 1806–1807, created by the long campaign of those years, when Napoleon's fate seemed in doubt. The Bank of France is still the central financial institution of the country, though it was nationalized in 1945.

Fiscal administration was directed by Michel Gaudin, later a duke. A sinking fund—a cash reserve available to guarantee the government's debts—was established. Part of the debt was repudiated; the rest drew regular interest. The government never failed to meet its obligations until the very last days of the regime.

For the general public, Napoleon went to a system of hard money—coin—altogether. Bank notes—minimum value 500 francs—were used by big business. Coin is always the most stable of currency.[6] He issued the franc de Germinal (5 grains of silver), which remained the standard in France for 123 years. Direct taxes were kept at a steady level; indirect taxes were adjusted upward as needed. The latter—sales taxes, license fees, and the like—were inequitable, but caused less opposition because they were paid piecemeal.

The administration was purged of useless officials and was centralized; there was rigorous auditing of books at every level. "The discovery of a dishonest accountant is a victory for the administration," preached Napoleon. The result of these policies was that the French complained little, though taxes were the highest in Europe, including countries conquered by Napoleon. The franc was the most stable currency in Europe, including Great Britain, during the period.

Napoleon continued the protectionist tariff policies of the Directory. They were directed primarily at Britain. The British, in turn, except in 1802–1803, ruined French overseas commerce. Napoleon ultimately countered with the Continental System (1806), an attempt to ban British goods from all of Europe (see pp. 67–68). Tariff arrangements benefited France, however, even at the expense of its satellites. Silk manufacturing at Lyons, for example, prospered at the expense of the Cisalpine Republic (later the Kingdom of Italy). There were high import duties on Italian cloth, low duties—ultimately none—on raw silk; export duties were nil on French cloth going to Italy. French manufacturers had no competition at home, therefore, and took over part of the Italian market as well. Only Italian manufactures which the French could not produce—certain laces, velours, and gauze—found a market in France. Despite discrimination against Italy and other countries, however, European industry expanded, and will be explained elsewhere.

All else possible was done to promote industry. Loans were made to French industries at low rates, and grants were

---

[6] Inflation with hard money can only occur through increase in the money supply, a debasement of the coinage, or an increase in the worldwide supply of gold and silver, reducing the market value.

made to some, especially new industries. Tax rebates and other devices were also used. Prizes were offered to inventors.

In agriculture and commerce, public works helped. Napoleon's engineers built or repaired some 50,000 miles of roads. The figure includes some roads that ran out of France proper, however. Every village, no matter how remote, was benefited. The extinction of robber bands was a great boon to commerce also—agricultural and otherwise. Subsidies were given for new crops. Sugar beets were the most successful of these. Beet sugar made up for a shortage of colonial cane sugar. Others included chicory, tobacco, cotton. A concerted attempt was made to improve herds by the importation of prize breeding stock from outside the country. For example, Spanish merinos were brought in and selectively mixed with French flocks. The result was sheep producing wool of better quality than either merino or the previous variety. Expansion of the wool cloth industry was a by-product.

Workers were required to carry the *livret* (work card-passport). Their employment was recorded, but their performance was not rated. They could change jobs at will, therefore, without prejudice, at least on the official record. The *livret* was issued to give protection to those gainfully employed. Those without one were assumed to be vagrants or bandits, and committed to workhouses or prison until proved otherwise. The *livret* contributed to keeping track of the work force, maintaining full employment—through the workhouses at last resort—and apprehending undesirables, criminals, and draft dodgers.

The methods of Napoleon were brutal, but the problems of beggary and banditry were very serious, and combating them required severe measures. Under the Directory, during one investigation of theft and murder, 400 "brigands" were imprisoned at Chartres, and perhaps 600 professional beggars interrogated and released.

Workers had the advantage of employment bureaus, established country-wide. These transferred people from areas of low employment to places where jobs were available. Britain, where the Industrial Revolution started much earlier than in France, had nothing similar until 1909. Labor unions were forbidden under the Le Chapelier Law of 1791, which remained in effect. There were, however, labor-management committees, required by the government and supervised thereby. It is true that only senior workers conferred with the managers, but at least grievances were aired. How much voice do junior workers have in labor unions today?

What were the overall results of the fiscal-economic policies? There was a growth of 25 percent in French industry; in metallurgy the percentage was higher. Much new industry was established—in metals, wool, sugar refining, tobacco processing, and even cotton, despite the blockade. Canning—food preserving in glass jars, vacuum sealed—was invented by one Nicholas Appert. Napoleon's armies were the first in the world to use canned food. There was full employment except for short periods in 1806–1807 and 1810–1811. Labor was so short that an unprecedented number of women—and, unhappily, children—were hired.

Several factors contributed to full employment: increased European markets, favorable tariffs, industrial growth, the demands of war, and an expanding population. Finally, conscription tended to drain off surplus manpower. Its effects, however, should not be exaggerated. Only 2,300,000 men were drafted during the fourteen years of Napoleon's power. Of these, 1,000,-000 were called in 1813–1814. Over the whole period 1800–1814, in the average department less than 3 percent of the population was displaced.

There was expansion in agriculture as well. Growing population and the needs of war served to keep prices up. The peasantry was prosperous; more peasants acquired land then before. This is one reason, at least, why the farmers were Napoleonists, though their sons did most of the dying in the imperial armies.

For the long run, it may be said that the Industrial Revolution truly got under way in France during the Napoleonic period. The same can be said of some other European countries under French control or influence for all or part of the period. The German states, for example, had a higher industrial growth rate than France—about 30 percent. Italian industry gained as well.

ADMINISTRATION AND JUDICIARY   Napoleon also reorganized the administrative-local government system. He took the basic pattern established by the National Assembly early in the Revolution, when 83 departments replaced the 34 intendancies (roughly equivalent to provinces). Departments were divided in descending order into districts *(arrondissements)*, cantons, and communes (municipalities). Officials in the local governments, except under the Terror, had been elected. Napoleon appointed prefects of departments, subprefects of districts, and the mayors of cities—those with over 5000 people directly; the smaller ones through the prefects.[7] These people were usually, but not always, chosen from local electoral lists. The departmental and district councils (advisory) were also appointed from Paris. Similar arrangements applied to the prefects and commissioners of police. The minister of police was head of both regular and secret police. The administrative system persists today, though mayors are now elected. Police centralization is perpetuated in the Sûreté.

A reorganization of the judiciary was also effected. All judges were appointed. Supervising the system were the chancellor (Jean Cambacérès after 1804) and the Council of State; the latter interpreted the law, a power later shared with the emperor's privy council. In the court system, the Court of Cassation stood at the top. It had civil and criminal jurisdiction, but did not decide cases or interpret the laws. It merely reviewed the records of lower courts, sending cases back for retrial where there had been legal or procedural error. Beneath it were civil and criminal systems. Both terminated at the lowest level with the justice(s) of the peace in the canton. In between were civil courts of first instance—one per district—and civil appeals courts—one per two or three departments—plus criminal courts—one per department. The system is essentially that of France today, though, of course, vastly expanded.

The Napoleonic administrative, judicial, and military

[7] The prefects were absolute governors of their departments. They were furnished detailed instructions from Paris, however, and ordered to follow them "literally." *Correspondance de Napoléon*, 5378 (February 15, 1802).

coteries have been the stabilizing factors in French government ever since 1815. Governments, parliaments, kings, another emperor, and presidents and their ministries have come and gone. The *fonctionnaires,* the civil servants, have gone on "forever," each generation replacing the last.

THE LAW CODES Napoleon was also responsible for the codification of the French law; in all, seven codes were produced. The first and most important was the civil code, called the Code Napoléon. It was worked out by a commission supervised by Cambacérès. Napoleon's personal influence on the code, however, is undoubted. He presided at 57 of the 102 meetings of the commission. Further, his notes appear throughout the drafts, and his ideas are apparent in the laws.

The civil code guaranteed individual liberty, stated certain rights such as equality before the law and in taxation, freedom from arrest without due process, religious freedom, and the right to choose one's work. It confirmed the abolition of feudalism in all its aspects, including corporate privilege such as had been held by guilds and cities. The most interesting features applied to property, marriage and divorce, and the rights of women.

There was to be equal division of property among all legitimate heirs—except that an individual might dispose of up to one-quarter by bequest. This was less radical than the revolutionary law providing for division of all without exception. Still, it made for the redistribution of property in each generation and the breaking up of great estates.

Civil marriage was required. Even if married in a church, couples had to go through a civil ceremony, thus registering the marriage with the state. Otherwise the churches (in most cases the Catholic) would still have to certify to the legitimacy of some heirs. Divorce was allowed by mutual consent. Other grounds were adultery, "excesses," conviction of a criminal offense of one party, or insanity. In any case the parties could not remarry for three years.

Obtaining a divorce was difficult. The law was written to help keep the family together. Women were at a disadvantage in these cases. In adultery, for example, if a wife caught her husband *en flagrante delicto* and shot him (and/or his partner), she was a murderess. If the husband, under reversed circumstances, caught his wife abed with a lover and shot one or both, no charge was possible against him. Moreover, catching a wife in adultery one time was sufficient for divorce, whereas the husband had to move a mistress into the home to have the charge proved.

Women were under other disabilities as well—"less equal than men." Their property had to be managed by a husband or male relative. In lawsuits, they were treated as if they were minors—with the protection and disadvantages attached thereto. In civil cases the courts were sympathetic, but women's testimony was taken lightly. In criminal cases where, for example, there were lurid details, women's testimony was taken in closed court —to protect their tender sensibilities.

The French law was not amended to give women reasonable equality until the 1960s. It was 1965 before the divorce law was rewritten, and 1966 before women were allowed to own businesses and have checking accounts. Naturally, women, being adept at subterfuge, had for decades actually been handling money and doing business.

The other major code was the Criminal Code. It specified equality before the law, equality in penalties, and forbade arbitrary arrest and imprisonment. Jury trial could be had in major cases at the request of the defendant. Torture by the police was allowed—under judicial restraint. This meant, in practice, that the police were rather brutal, especially to persons thought dangerous or habitual offenders. They also had the right to hold persons in custody, under warrant, for almost unlimited periods. The prosecution, in all cases, had more rights than the defense. The defense, for example, had to apprise the prosecution and judges of all witnesses and evidence it expected to bring before the court; the prosecution was not so hampered. Further, the judges could order new trials if juries ruled "illegally." For those brought up in the tradition of English and American law this seems incredible. To the French, with their inbred respect for authority of the qualified, it seemed normal—and still does.

The French law did not, and does not, presume persons guilty until proved innocent. It was, however, written to protect the state, not the individual. The feeling was that it was better for innocents to be punished than for society to suffer. The assumption of American law, based on the English law, has always been the opposite.

There were five other codes: commercial, of civil procedure, of criminal instruction, penal, and rural.

For the first time all of France had the same laws; all provincial variations were nullified. The codes preserved the ideals of the Revolution while incorporating a comfortable measure of the traditional. The Code Napoléon, especially, was not a synthesis of local law, but "cut from whole cloth" by experts and imposed by authority, like the Roman law, which Napoleon so revered.

The Napoleonic codes, expanded and amended, remain the basic law of France; they have also influenced the law of most European countries and that of many other parts of the world.

EDUCATION In education, Napoleon's influence is often decried, but he left a lasting legacy. As to public schools, he turned the primary system, in effect, back to the church, though municipal and private schools were allowed. He eliminated the secondary "central schools" of the Directory (one per department), and had no interest in reviving the Terrorists' plan for free public schools. To replace the "central schools," he established 45 *lycées* (roughly, high schools) and allowed private, mostly church, *collèges* on the same level.

The purpose of the *lycées* was to train future officers and civil servants. Headmasters and administrative boards were appointed by Napoleon. Inspectors general visited each at least once a year. There were 6400 scholarships available, of which 2400 went to the sons of officers and civil servants, the remainder to the "best" students of lower schools. The curriculum included classical languages, rhetoric, morality, logic, mathematics, and science. The *lycées* were under military and clerical discipline. Both the *lycées* and *collèges* adopted the baccalaureate examination for graduation. This exam persists in France today. Now, as then, one cannot go on to a university or one of the "Great Schools," without passing it. Every year, students still cram and work themselves into states of near-hysteria over the "bacs."

Napoleon preserved the *Grandes Écoles* (Great Schools) established by the Convention. The principal ones were the École Polytechnique and the École Normale Supérieure. The Polytechnic trained engineers—civil and military—though graduates had to enter the army or navy in the latter years of the Empire. The Normal School trained teachers and research men in science and the humanities. Graduation from either guaranteed a career in government service, or, generally, elsewhere, if desired.

The Great Schools still enjoy the highest prestige in France. New ones have been founded, notably the National School of Administration (1945) to train prospective *fonctionnaires*. Prior to its creation the École Polytechnique, despite its origin as an engineering school, produced the most cabinet ministers and other high officials. The two now share about equal rank. The tradition of elitism is still very much alive in theory and in practice. Any talented child of the provinces, however, has a chance to get into the Great Schools. Napoleon also must have credit for establishing the chief military academy of France, Saint-Cyr, although he had the old École Militaire, as modified by the revolutionary governments, to build on.

The Institut de France, also founded by the Convention, was preserved. It was an honorific body, but also directed to the collection of knowledge and research. Originally it had three sections. Napoleon organized it into four; physical and mathematical sciences, French language and literature (the Académie Française), history and literature, and fine arts. He had political motive in reorganizing it, as mentioned earlier. But the Institut survived, though the Académie Française was suppressed temporarily in 1811. It is very much alive today.[8]

[8] The Institut de France now has five sections: the Académie Française, the Académie des Inscriptions et Belles-Lettres, the Académie des Sciences, the Académie des Beaux-Arts, and the Académie des Sciences Morales et Politiques.

To insure control of education, Napoleon organized the Imperial University. Not a university in the ordinary sense, it was a corporation of all the professors and teachers in France, who were required to be members. It was headed by a Grand Master, Louis de Fontanes, who was advised by a council of 30 educators. He was in charge of standardizing education in France from the universities to the primary schools. The University—really its Grand Master and Council—specified the curricula, chose the texts, specified the nature of examinations and when and where they were to be held, and even the system of grading. Everyone who stood on a platform in France was put under discipline—from the dons of the Sorbonne to the village schoolmasters. The University continued to operate in France until 1850. Some organization of the sort, under the minister of education, has existed ever since.

Only the education of women remained outside the purview of the University. Napoleon took little interest in it. Most girls, he opined, could be educated best by their mothers. Their role was private, not public. He did authorize the opening of a finishing school, for girls of the upper classes, in the château of Écouen, and took time to dictate instructions for its operation in the midst of the 1807 campaign. Teach them good French, he wrote, a little arithmetic, geography, history, and a smattering of science. But three-quarters of their time should be spent learning sewing, "other female occupations," and good grooming. Religion and manners, though, were really all they needed to learn.[9]

Napoleon has been damned for gearing the educational system to produce soldiers and civil servants and to indoctrinate the young in loyalty to the regime. At least he made no pretense of doing otherwise. "My object in establishing a teaching corps (the University)," he told the Council of State, "is to have a means of directing political and moral opinion."[10] He also said that without "a public instruction . . . there is no equality [for the common man] except that of misery and servitude."[11] But

[9] *Correspondance de Napoléon*, 12585 (May 15, 1807).
[10] Napoléon, *Pensées*, p. 49 (February 20, 1806).
[11] *Correspondance de Napoléon*, 6591 (February 29, 1806).

"public instruction" for him meant education by the state for the public good. He was determined that the church would never regain its ancient monopoly.

Napoleon succeeded in preserving secular direction of education, though the church has always played a major role in it. Moreover, his mark is apparent today on the French school system—at every level.

CULTURAL LIFE   Related to education, Napoleon preserved and expanded the Bibliothèque Nationale (National Library). The Archives Nationales were given a new home in 1804—the Palace de Rohan-Soubise—where they are still located. Napoleon also must have credit for making the Louvre one of the world's great art museums—perhaps today the greatest. To accomplish this he brought art treasures from all over Europe. But they were not "stolen," as is often alleged. The Allies, after Napoleon's defeat, decided that most of them had been purchased or otherwise legally acquired, if in abnormal situations. Some were returned to their former owners, including the famous horses of St. Mark's, Venice. Most of those which left the Louvre, however, were bought from the restored Bourbon government. The man who set the pattern was Tsar Alexander I. Many of the paintings and objects that now grace the Hermitage, in Leningrad (formerly St. Petersburg), were shipped from Paris in 1814–1815.

Much has been made of the exile of Madame de Staël and Benjamin Constant. But one wonders if much of their fame was not a result of it. Surely Constant produced nothing of world-shaking value. Chateaubriand,[12] in France, published *Le génie du Christianism* (1802), his most famous work, and *Les Martyrs* (1809), though he was denied a seat in the Académie Française.

---

[12] The Viscount François-René de Chateaubriand (1768–1848) was a royalist who returned from exile after Brumaire. The *Génie,* published after the Concordat, was dedicated "to the present government." He broke with Napoleon in 1803, however. (See p. 40.) Author of many works, he is usually named as the founder of the romantic school in France. He wrote against Napoleon in 1814, but his *Mémoires d'outre tombe* (1849–50) reflect a deep nostalgia for France's era of glory.

The verse of Jacques Delille, official poet of the Empire, was praised even by Madame de Staël.

Marie-Joseph Chénier, an outstanding dramatist, was an inspector of the Imperial University. René de Pixérécourt, "father of the melodrama," set trends that lasted a century. The stage was graced by Talma, one of the greatest tragedians of all time. The Marquis de Sade, whose *Justine* has become a classic, if pornographic, was in the mental hospital at Charenton (his family approved) but wrote and produced plays to which the public was admitted. The theater and opera were very active. Napoleon patronized and regularly attended both. He loved the classics of Corneille, Racine, Molière—particularly the trage-dies, and new plays on classic, especially ancient, themes. Of the new, his favorite was *Les Templiers* of François Raynouard.

The emperor had a traveling library of 1000 books, which he took on campaign. It comprised 660 histories and historical memoirs, together with poetry, drama, novels, and religious works. Included (in translation) were Henry Fielding's *Tom Jones,* Samuel Richardson's *Pamela,* and classics from Homer, Lucan, and Tasso to Rousseau and Montesquieu. The works of living authors he accepted or rejected, tossing those he dis-liked out his carriage window. His great favorite was *The Poems of Ossian,* translated by Letourneur, which even became the basis for an opera, with music by Jean François Lesueur. We do not know what he thought of the early efforts of Sten-dhal. The leading novelist of the day was Ducray-Duminil, whose books are still read.

In art, it is only necessary to mention the names of Jacques David, Antoine Gros, Pierre-Paul Prud'hon, Géricault, and J.-B. Wicar. In Italy, Antonio Canova was patronized by Napo-leon, and in Spain, Goya. The Empire set a style in painting, sculpture, architecture, furniture, and dress which is distinc-tive; in literature the romantic period began.

Doubtless, the scientists were Napoleon's favorites. The Empire boasted great names: Gaspard Monge, the father of descriptive geometry, Louis Joseph Lagrange, another mathe-matician of genius, Pierre-Simon Laplace, whose *Mécanique Céleste* pioneered in astronomy, and the zoologist Jean Baptiste

Lamarck. Napoleon fostered the work of the physicists Karl Friedrich Gauss, in Germany, and Alessandro Volta in Italy.

Repression of political expression there was. But those who say Napoleon created an intellectual desert in France and Europe are wrong.

PUBLIC WORKS   Napoleon left monuments and public works. The centerpiece of Paris, the Arc de Triomphe, was almost completed in 1814. The Arc du Carrousel and the column of the Place Vendôme were in place, among hundreds of other lesser monuments. Almost completed too was the Church of the Madeleine, begun by Louis XV, a shrine of the men of the Grande Armée. Some projects, mercifully, were never finished, for example that of a huge elephant, spouting water, for the Place de la Bastille. New bridges were thrown across the Seine. Paris got a fresh water supply, via a new canal from the Ourcq River. To the chagrin of water peddlers, fountains flowed day and night in all quarters. The city sewer system was reconstructed. A number of streets were straightened and widened. The French canal system was extended by some 200 kilometers, though the major project, connecting the Rhone and the Rhine, was not finished. We have earlier noted the roads built in France; many routes extended beyond, notably the spectacular highway across the Mt. Cenis Pass of the Alps to Italy, and the Corniche, cut into the bluffs of the French and Italian Rivieras. Hardly a village is without reminders of Napoleon—practical and decorative.

CONCLUSION   "I am so much identified with our . . . monuments, or institutions, all our national acts, that one would not know how to separate me from them. . . ." said the fallen emperor in 1816. It has been true ever since: it is true today. It is patent that the Napoleonic genius still guides France through the Code Napoléon, the judiciary, and administration; the Bank of France still operates. Napoleon's spirit pervades education. The Louvre museum is as much his monument as the Invalides. When the "immortals" of the Académie Française turn out, it is a modified version of the uniform Napoleon had the French painter David design for them. In their insistence on constitutional government, flatly contradicted by their disdain for legislative babblers, the French maintain the emperor's own attitude. French preference for elitist leadership antedates Napoleon, as does French passion for centralized government and national planning. But he certainly brought these back into vogue with a verve Louis XIV would have approved.

Moreover, the most successful French leaders since Napoleon's time have emulated him. There was an echo of his rhetoric in that of Charles de Gaulle. Said Napoleon, "My policy is to govern the people as the great number desires. That . . . is the way to recognize the sovereignty of the people." Said De Gaulle: "[My government] . . . is the system of the national majority . . . of that which emerges from the nation as a whole, expressing itself through its undivided and sovereign mass." Napoleon: "Let the legislature have the power to stop the march of government in its details—and that would result [in enfeeblement]. . . ." De Gaulle: "Under [the previous Republic] . . . the Parliament . . . [was] the exclusive source of power. . . . Such a system was not normally able to . . . accomplish all the firm and constant designs that constitute a policy, nor, all the more . . . [to lead] France in the major contemporary dramas."[13]

Never has the influence of one man been so persistent in the institutions and life of a nation as of Napoleon in France.

[13] Napoleon's words from messages to the Council of State. Napoléon, *Pensées,* p. 30 (July 4, 1800) and p. 35 (February 1804); de Gaulle's from press conference of November 9, 1965. *Speeches and Press Conferences,* No. 228 (New York: Ambassade de France; Service de Presse et d'Information, 1965). See also Miot, *Mémoires,* I, p. 325, where Napoleon says if "public opinion" supports the legislative bodies against him, he will have no choice but to "renounce governing" —something de Gaulle did twice, in 1946 and 1969.

CHAPTER FOUR

The Empire

NAPOLEONIC WARFARE This chapter covers the building of the Empire; the next the administration of its states. Since the route to Empire was one of war, a short note is in order here about Napoleon's army, strategy, and tactics.

The standing army, from 1805 on, comprised about 600,000 men. Its officers and noncommissioned officers were largely professionals; the ranks were filled by conscripts—men between twenty and twenty-five, the youngest called first. There were hardship exemptions and one could "buy" a substitute. As noted earlier (p. 45) draft quotas were not very high until 1812–1814. Napoleon normally took the field with about 200,000 French (reinforced with contingents from allied and satellite states). Of these, about 130,000 were infantry, 30,000 to 40,000 cavalry, 20,000 artillery, and the rest engineers and other support troops.

The basic unit-of-all-arms was the corps of 20,000 to 30,000 men, commanded by a marshal or lieutenant general, broken down into 2 to 4 infantry divisions, with cavalry, artillery, and support units. Usually, the corps was backed by 6 to 8 companies of artillery, with 6 cannon and 2 howitzers (huge, high-angle mortars) each—or a total of 48 to 64 guns. They were in close support of infantry, since the range averaged about one-half mile, maximum. Always present were units of the Imperial Guard, the emperor's trump card.

The Guard, which numbered 60,000 by 1812, was a small army in itself, with its own infantry, cavalry, artillery, and train. Part of it was often detached, for example, for service in Spain. The men were all combat veterans of long service. Privates ranked with sergeants of the line; sergeants-major with lieutenants; colonels were generals of the regular army. The emperor himself usually wore the uniform of colonel of Guard cavalry. After 1809, when the Young Guard was formed, the Old Guard regiments were hardly ever committed in battle. Though mostly French, the Guard also had regiments of Poles, Germans, Italians, and others, and a company of Mamelukes.

In general, French tactics can be described. On the defense, they used the three- or two-man line. In the attack, the infantry carried the burden, jogging forward in battalion column—800 to 900 men with a 60-man front. They were preceded by skirmishers *(voltigeurs),* who advanced, Indian-fashion, taking cover as it appeared, sniping at the enemy and disrupting his formations. The columns charged, shouting, bugles blowing, delivering volleys of fire. Their object was to break through the enemy line and open flanks. Cavalry followed up to widen the gaps and attack the enemy rear. Artillery was used throughout to disorganize the opponent. These tactics worked well against continental armies, but not against the British, especially under Wellington, whose veteran marksmen stood steady and decimated the column.

Napoleon's personal tactics defy analysis. He never fought two battles the same way. (We shall describe several below). His rule was "Engage and then see what develops." He normally held back a large part of his army until the pattern of enemy action became clear. Then his remarkable intuition came into

Some of Napoleon's twenty-six marshals. They include Murat, king of Naples, 1808–1815; Berthier, the emperor's almost indispensable chief-of-staff; Marmont, sometime governor of Illyria; Ney, the "bravest of the brave"; and Masséna and Soult, both great field commanders. *(The New York Public Library)*

play. Sensing the opponent's weak point, he would hurl overwhelming force against it at just the right time—artillery blast-
ing, the infantry rolling forward, and the cavalry moving in for
the *coup de grâce*. Never, however, did he leave himself without
a reserve, at least the Old Guard—until Waterloo. His mere
presence was important—worth 40,000 men, said Wellington.
When a French unit wavered, he could be counted on to appear,
and the men took heart. They had come to believe that "the
cannon ball has not been cast that can kill the Emperor," and he
was with them.

Napoleon used more guns, and massed their fire better,
than any other commander had before. His artillery, however,
was inherited from the Old Regime—4-, 6-, 8-, and 12-pound
guns and 6-inch howitzers—smooth bore, muzzle loading—the
best in Europe. His column attack formation, though refined,
he took from the revolutionary armies, who had devised it to
control raw troops. It kept them together, bolstered morale,
and allowed men who were not marksmen to deliver a hail of
fire in the right general direction. His genius was displayed
not in great innovation as to arms, organization, or basic tactics,
but in his use of the proper "mix" of units and combination of
defense and attack to fit the situation.

The emperor's strategy is easier to describe. Basing his
orders on the careful work of Marshal Alexandre Berthier and
his staff, he moved his army forward along all available parallel
routes to concentrate the greatest number of men and weapons
at a given place at the proper time. His weak point was supply.
"The war must feed the war," he said. The troops lived off the
land as necessary. Before a campaign, however, he advanced
depots for supplies, food, weapons, and ammunition as far forward as conditions allowed. And on his perpetual fronts—the
Elbe in Germany, the Bug in Poland, the feet of the Alpine passes in Italy—he always kept the fortresses heavily stocked for
future action.

PRELUDE TO WAR Napoleon treated the Peace of Amiens (1802)
as a truce. He kept French markets closed to the British and
forced Spain, an ally since 1795, and the sister republics to limit

theirs. He attempted to revive the French Empire in America. More alarming to George III's government, however, he extended French power on the Mediterranean shores.

In 1802 he annexed Piedmont and Elba, which had just been evacuated by the British, to France, took over Parma-Piacenza, and was "elected" president of the Italian (formerly Cisalpine) Republic. His agents were at work in the Ottoman empire and Egypt. He kept garrisons in Naples (until 1805) and impaired British commerce.

Not strangely, the British refused to give up Malta, as agreed at Amiens, but offered to negotiate. Napoleon replied with insults, and Britain declared war in May 1803.

Napoleon immediately seized Hanover, a possession of George III, extending his power to the center of Germany. In 1803 also the reorganization of Germany, agreed to at Lunéville, destroyed 112 small states and expanded larger ones, all to the disadvantage of the Austrian Holy Roman Emperor, Francis II. (See pp. 29–30.) Russia's new tsar, Alexander I, concerned over French influence in the Baltic, restored trade with Britain, and leaned toward an alliance.

In 1804 the powers were further shaken by the legalized murder of the Duc d'Enghien. (See p. 33.) Genoa was closed to British ships, and shortly annexed to France. Spain reluctantly declared war on Britain. Finally, Napoleon took the title of Emperor, a particular blow to Francis II of Austria. (See p. 35.)

KINGDOM OF ITALY   In 1805 Napoleon made himself king of Italy, usurping another Habsburg title. And Russia now saw its Balkan interests clearly menaced.

The Kingdom of Italy was another incarnation of the Italian Republic, which had been ruled for President Bonaparte by its vice-president, Francesco Melzi, an aristocratic Francophile. He was replaced by a viceroy, Josephine's son, Eugène de Beauharnais, now a tall, young cavalry officer. In May 1805 Napoleon crowned himself in the Cathedral of Milan with the "Iron Crown" of the ancient Lombard kings, and assumed their style, "Rex Totius Italiae" (King of all Italy). This act alarmed the pope and the Bourbons of Naples. The success of the coronation disturbed them further. Some 30,000 people jammed the cathedral; more thousands waited outside to cheer.

Russia had allied with Britain in April 1805; Austria joined the coalition in August. The pope lent moral support to the Allies. Naples allied with France, but the sincerity of Queen Marie Caroline was questionable. "New Attila" and "Corsican Bastard" were only two of her terms of "affection" for Napoleon.

TRAFALGAR   Since 1803 Napoleon had been building an army at Boulogne, ostensibly to invade England. Surely, however, by 1805, he was not serious about it. If he managed to cross the Channel with an army—a chancy business—he might conquer England (British land forces were very small) but lose France to his enemies on the Continent. In Italy he had alerted the army for Austrian attack, inspected the fortresses, and sent Marshal André Masséna to assist Eugène de Beauharmais. His attention was on Europe, not England.

To confuse his enemies, however, he continued his invasion sham, taking command at Boulogne on August 3, 1805. The game lost him his major fleet, under Admiral Pierre Villeneuve, which was driven from the Channel and later destroyed by Admiral Nelson off Cape Trafalgar. But the sideshow enabled him to surprise the Austrians in Germany.

Trafalgar (October 1808) established Britian as mistress of the seas and enabled it to wage war continually until Napoleon fell in 1814. But in 1805 the significance of the battle was not so clear. The news of it was almost lost amid reports of the triumphs of the Grande Armée.[1]

CAMPAIGN OF 1805   On August 22 Napoleon had ordered Villeneuve, all too publicly: "Enter the channel, England is ours. . . ." Actually units of the "Army of England" were already en route to Germany. Austrian armies, which entered Germany on September 11, found Napoleon upon them weeks before they expected him.

---

[1] When the emperor was in command, any French army became the Grande Armée.

At the end of September the Grande Armée was across the Rhine, 200,000 strong, including 20,000 Imperial Guards. Napoleon's generals were men who would make legend: Joachim Murat, the giant, proud Gascon horseman; Michel Ney, the "bravest of the brave," a tall, red-haired, vain Saarlander; Bernadotte, the future king of Sweden; Nicolas Soult, small, wiry, dynamic; Louis Davout, the "bald eagle," tall, broad-shouldered, a humorless professional. The chief-of-staff was Alexandre Berthier, a severe, swarthy, little gamecock.

The Austrian vanguard, under General Mack, was caught at Ulm and captured (October 15); the other Allied forces scattered. Napoleon drove straight for Vienna, picking up 100,-000 troops of German allies as he marched. He ignored the Austrian campaign in Italy. "I will lead the enemy in such a dance . . ." he wrote Eugène, "that he will have not time to bother you. . . ." This proved true. The Grande Armée, Murat's cavalry in the lead, took Vienna in November.

The Russian army had arrived late and retreated into Moravia. Tsar Alexander I, young, full of energy, took command. Francis of Austria joined him with a few troops. Alexander had been reared at the castle of his drillmaster father—where his mentor, a tough sergeant, had leave to beat him—and at the court of his grandmother, Catherine the Great, where he was pampered and dosed with French "philosophy." He was alternately despot and *philosophe*. In either mood he fancied himself a soldier. He looked the part, at least—blond, tall, muscular, and superbly uniformed.

Napoleon moved into Moravia also and dispersed his corps for provisioning. This encouraged the Tsar to attack. His generals urged him to wait for the Archduke Charles who, half expecting Napoleon in Italy, had attacked there but was now rapidly marching northward. Alexander, however, for the moment, had Napoleon outnumbered—87,000 to 73,000. He decided to fight.

On December 2, near Austerlitz, the tsar attacked Napoleon's seemingly weak south flank, hoping to cut him off from Vienna. But his troops stalled in the icy marshes and wave after wave was cut to pieces. Napoleon let the Russians bleed, then,

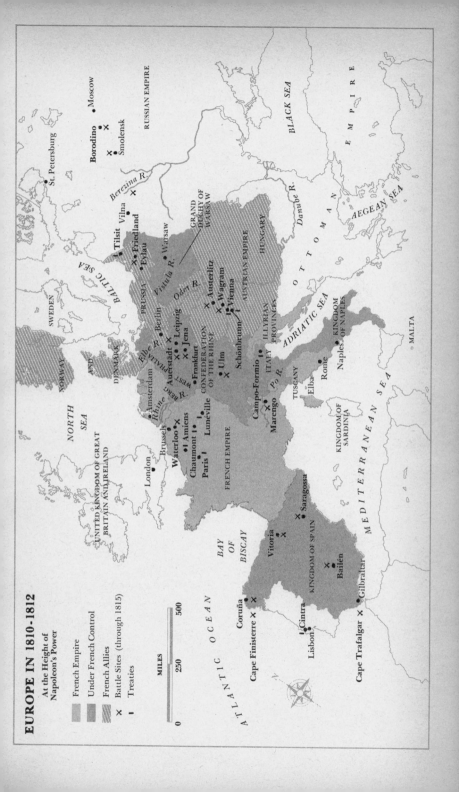

EUROPE IN 1810-1812

At the Height of
Napoleon's Power

French Empire
Under French Control
French Allies
Battle Sites (through 1815) X
Treaties

MILES
0   250   500

ATLANTIC OCEAN

UNITED KINGDOM OF GREAT
BRITAIN AND IRELAND

London

NORTH
SEA

NORWAY

SWEDEN

Amsterdam
Brussels
Rhine R.
BERG
WESTPHALIA
Auerstädt X
Elbe R.
Berlin
PRUSSIA
Tilsit
Friedland X
Eylau X
Vilna
Berezina R. X
Moscow
Borodino X X Smolensk
St. Petersburg
RUSSIAN EMPIRE

BALTIC SEA

DENMARK

Waterloo X
Chaumont
Paris
Amiens
Lunéville
FRENCH EMPIRE

Frankfurt
CONFEDERATION
OF THE RHINE
Leipzig
Jena X
Ulm X
Schönbrunn
Austerlitz X
Wagram X
Vienna
AUSTRIAN EMPIRE
HUNGARY
Oder R.
Vistula R.
Warsaw
GRAND
DUCHY OF
WARSAW

Danube R.

BLACK SEA

AEGEAN SEA

OTTOMAN EMPIRE

Campo-Formio
Marengo
Po R.
ITALY
Rome
ILLYRIAN
PROVINCES
TUSCANY
Elba
KINGDOM OF NAPLES
Naples

ADRIATIC SEA

MEDITERRANEAN SEA

MALTA

BAY
OF
BISCAY

Cape Finisterre X
Coruña X
Vitoria X
Saragossa X
KINGDOM OF SPAIN
Bailén X X
Gibraltar X
Cintra
Lisbon
Cape Trafalgar X

KINGDOM OF
SARDINIA

in midafternoon, hurled the weight of his army on the tsar's north flank, turning it and driving the enemy south into swamps, streams, and lakes. The remnants fled, the tsar among them.

Austria, but not Russia, made peace at Pressburg on December 26, 1805. Austria lost Venice and Venetian Istria and Dalmatia to Italy. Napoleon's allies, the dukes of Bavaria and Württemberg, were made kings and were ceded Austrian territory. Bavaria received the Tyrol, Vorarlberg, and Augsburg. Habsburg lands in Swabia were turned over to Württemberg. It was a harsh settlement. Surely it made an even more implacable enemy of Austria.

NAPLES "The dynasty of Naples has ceased to reign," Napoleon proclaimed after Austerlitz. Queen Marie Caroline had finally gone too far. She was the real ruler; her fat, easy-going husband, Ferdinand—"the Nose"—was completely under her thumb.[2] Though allied with France, she had allowed a British-Russian force to land in Naples; it withdrew after Austerlitz. Marie pled for mercy. The "Emperor of all Europe" must know, she wrote Napoleon, that the Allies had forced themselves upon her. He thought that droll. "I will finally fix that whore," he told Talleyrand. Already Masséna was marching on Naples with 40,000 men.

In January 1806 Joseph Bonaparte was dispatched from Paris to assume the "vacant" throne. He had been recalcitrant over the creation of the Empire. "Prince Égalité," Napoleon had called him. But he accepted the crown of Naples after the emperor promised him a free hand in governing and threatened to "disinherit" him if he refused.[3]

The conquest of Naples was a walkover. The Bourbon king and queen fled to Sicily; their armies swiftly followed. Most of the nobles and the middle class remained to welcome the French, anxious that Joseph's army enter quickly and insure

[2] The Bourbon queen was a Habsburg by birth, sister of the guillotined queen of France, Marie Antoinette.

[3] Joseph's rights in the imperial succession were also guaranteed. This represented a new turn in Napoleon's thinking. Thereafter his rulers all had dual citizenship, and would, he hoped, place France first in their allegiance.

their property against notorious *lazzaroni* (city proletariat) of Naples. Only the fortress of Gaeta, under the bomb-shaped, hard-drinking Prince of Hesse-Philippsthal, held out (until July). The British landed 5000 men, under Sir John Stuart, in the south, who disrupted the French occupation. But Stuart got little support from the Neapolitan guerrillas, to whom he represented the hated Bourbons.[4] He withdrew.

Meanwhile Joseph entered his capital in mid-February 1806 through triumphal arches. The city fathers greeted him; the clergy celebrated with a *Te Deum* at the Cathedral of Saint Januarius, patron saint of Naples. The emperor, informed, snidely asked if he had also remembered to man the forts.

Joseph had seen to his defenses, but his mind was on other things. In early March he wrote Napoleon: "Death from starvation is common here . . . surely something can be done about it." He began wide-sweeping reforms that were beginning to bear fruit, when he was "transferred" to Spain (1808). The new rulers, Murat and his wife, Caroline Bonaparte, continued some of them.

HOLLAND   In 1806 Napoleon also converted the Batavian Republic into the Kingdom of Holland under his brother Louis. The Republic's Grand Pensionary, Rutger Jan Schimmelpenninck, had governed well and also supplied money and naval units to France. But he haggled over Dutch obligations to France, and argued that the Netherlands should be a vast free port—trading with all the world. France would both share the profits and have access to anything it needed—British and colonial goods included. To Napoleon the scheme was anathema, since it would also benefit the British.

When, in 1806, Schimmelpenninck began to go blind, the emperor had an excuse to change the government. His first impulse was to annex Holland to France. But that might alarm neutral Prussia and push King Frederick William into active alliance with the tsar. And Louis Bonaparte, Napoleon thought,

[4] The Bourbons, with popular support, had overthrown the French-sponsored Parthenopean Republic in 1799. But they had rewarded their people with repression.

would be easy to control. Earlier a spirited soldier, and still nominally an officer, he had taken to dreamy intellectualism and visiting the baths to nurse real or imagined ills.

Talleyrand informed the Dutch of Napoleon's plans for a kingdom. In April 1806 Schimmelpenninck assembled a "Great Committee"—his legislature and ministry—which, after attempts to negotiate with the emperor, was told to accept a constitutional monarchy or Holland would be annexed to France. On June 5 a Dutch delegation dutifully appeared in Paris and formally petitioned the emperor to create a kingdom under Louis Bonaparte. Napoleon gracefully acceded.

On June 15, 1806, Louis departed for the Hague. En route he proclaimed "I have changed my nationality." He meant it. Because he became so thoroughly Dutch, his reign was very short, but surprisingly productive.

WHY THE CHARADE? Why the deputation, request, and the rest? Didn't everybody know that Napoleon was forcing a new government on the Dutch? No, they didn't. News was controlled. The Dutch were told that their leaders had freely asked for a Bonaparte king. If rumor said otherwise, the public falsehood was easier to take. And Louis's presence might give Holland favor in Paris if not independence. He was the emperor's brother. For the crowned heads of Europe, also, it was convenient to accept the official fiction. Napoleon persisted in such charades, which gave an aura of legality to his actions and masked his use of force and threats.

CONFEDERATION OF THE RHINE In July 1806 Napoleon proclaimed himself Protector of the Confederation of the Rhine (Rheinbund), which soon comprised all the German states except Prussia. The Holy Roman Emperor, recognizing that he had been replaced in Germany by the Emperor of the French, abdicated his title and became simply Emperor of Austria.[5] The sympathy of Prussia was with Austria, though they had long been rivals in Germany.

[5] Francis II as Holy Roman Emperor, he became Francis I of Austria.

Prussia had other complaints. It had been given Hanover in 1805. But Frederick William learned that Napoleon was secretly offering Hanover to Britain in return for peace. The French emperor had already disposed of Prussian states given in exchange. Moreover, he had forced Prussia to stop trading with Britain. The Prussian king was humiliated and uncertain of the future. His antique military advisers meanwhile had convinced him the kingdom was strong. He acted as if it were the Prussia of Frederick the Great.

WAR AGAIN   Prussia allied with Russia in July 1806, mobilized in early August, and without waiting for its ally, marched on the Rheinbund. Frederick William hoped to surprise Napoleon and cause his German allies to defect. He did neither. The French emperor quickly struck back with an army of 260,000, one-fourth German. He was thirty-seven; Davout, his chief subordinate, was thirty-six. The Prussians had 125,000 effectives, led by the duke of Brunswick, seventy-one, and Prince Hohenlohe, another ancient warrior. The two hated each other, commanded an obsolete army, and coordinated nothing. On October 14 their forces were destroyed in twin battles at Jena and Auerstädt. What troops remained fled to the Russians, as did the king of Prussia and his court. The French took Berlin and marched east.

THE CONTINENTAL SYSTEM   By the Berlin Decree (November 1806), Napoleon initiated the Continental System, implying total control of Europe, which he had yet to win. British ships—or others originating at British, including colonial, ports—were banned from European ports. A blockade (which was unenforceable) of the British Isles was declared. All British goods were ordered confiscated. The emperor's object was to bankrupt the "nation of shopkeepers" by closing its principal market—Europe.

The British, who already had French and North Sea ports under real blockade, extended the blockade to all ports controlled by France or its allies. Neutral vessels complying with French regulations were fair prize. Napoleon replied with the

Milan Decree (December 1807), which made all ships forfeit that touched a British port or submitted to search by the royal navy.

After 1807 no nation could remain aloof from the French-British struggle. Thus the United States and other neutrals were affected, as well as colonial areas, notably Latin America. The Continental System did not break the British economy, but it gave it severe shocks, as we shall note later. It was a factor in driving Napoleon to overextend his power, but decidedly contributed to the growth of European industry.

FRIEDLAND   In the winter of 1806–1807 the French pursued the Russians, who steadfastly refused to fight, over the vast expanses of Poland and East Prussia. It was February 1807 before a major battle was fought—at Eylau—bloody but indecisive. In the spring the maneuvering speeded up.

In June 1807 the enemy made a fatal error. General Levin Bennigsen took the main Russian army (60,000) across the Alle River at Friedland—a slow all-night operation—to crush 10,000 French under Marshal Jean Lannes. But Napoleon rode hell-for-leather from Eylau, drew in 80,000 men, and attacked. Bennigsen could not get away. Driven through Friedland, which was set afire, and into the river, the Russians were butchered, drowned, and burned alive. Victory was complete.

TILSIT   The tsar and the king of Prussia made peace at Tilsit (July 7–9, 1807). Napoleon made an ally of the tsar, whom he met halfway—on a raft in the Niemen River—and completely charmed. He gave Russia a bit of East Prussia and talked of dividing control of Europe and partitioning Turkey between Russia and France. Alexander undertook to mediate peace between France and Britain, promising if he failed—and he did—to join the Continental System. Prussia joined the System, was assessed an indemnity, and had to support French occupation troops until it was paid. Prussian Poland became the Grand Duchy of Warsaw. Moreover, Prussia lost all territory west of the Elbe—a small part to the Grand Duchy of Berg, created for Murat in 1806, the rest to the new Kingdom of Westphalia.

THE GRAND DUCHY OF WARSAW   Warsaw was placed "temporarily" under Napoleon's ally, the king of Saxony.[6] It stood as an earnest to the Poles of the ultimate resurrection of the Kingdom of Poland—though Napoleon never said so. Some Poles had fought with the French since the partitions (the last 1795) had divided their country among Prussia, Russia, and Austria. General Jan Dombrowski's legions had distinguished themselves. The Polish cavalry of the Imperial Guard was noted for its valor.

In 1806 Prince Joseph Poniatowski, a dashing soldier of royal blood, rallied the Poles against the Russians. In 1807 most of the high nobility cast their lot with Napoleon. He had defeated all the partitioning powers. What better hope for Poland?

Poland continued to supply troops. It was the eastern bastion of the Empire until 1813, and many Poles fought with the French until the end. The Kingdom of Poland was not reconstituted by Napoleon, but a valiant attempt was made to give the Grand Duchy enlightened government.

WESTPHALIA   The Kingdom of Westphalia comprised Prussia east of the Elbe, its late allies, Brunswick and Hesse-Cassel, part of Hanover, and some lesser states. The crown went to the youngest Bonaparte, Jerome, fifteen years Napoleon's junior. Handsome, much indulged, he was perhaps Europe's most notorious playboy. He had served in the navy, however, with monumental insubordination but some valor, and as a general in the recent campaign. Napoleon admired his spirit and intelligence, but did not fully trust him.

With seeming illogic, the emperor nevertheless expected him to make Westphalia the model state of the Rheinbund. It was to have an active parliament, French-style administration and courts, and the Code Napoléon. To a surprising degree, Jerome molded the state to Napoleon's specifications. It served France well, and left an enduring legacy.

---

[6] The duke of Saxony was allied with Prussia until after Jena, then switched sides. Napoleon made him a king.

THE SPANISH ALLY Spain, defeated earlier by the French Republic, had been allied with France since 1795. The alliance had brought it nothing but grief. The British had ruined Spain's trade and cut off communications with its colonies. France had taken Santo Domingo and Louisiana, lost one and sold the other.[7] Charles IV had joined the Continental System, sent Napoleon troops, and owed millions in subsidy. His navy had been lost at Trafalgar. The Spanish economy was disrupted; the port cities were wracked by labor unrest and violence. Humiliated by the French, the Spanish equally damned their own leaders.

The government was dominated by Prince Manuel Godoy, first minister and commander of the army and navy. He was also the lover of the queen, Maria Louisa—aging, debauched, but forceful. She scorned Charles IV, who was mild mannered, a lover of the countryside, and at intervals insane. Ferdinand, the crown prince, intrigued constantly to seize the crown and ruin Godoy. In his early twenties, he was dumpy, with a low forehead and the jutting "Habsburg jaw." But to the people he was Prince Charming—and their only hope for reform. Many Spanish liberals also backed him, though earlier he had betrayed his followers to save himself. He was currently seeking a Bonaparte bride.

The Spanish government was in debt, inefficient, top-heavy with officials, and burdened with pensioners. The church was vastly overstaffed and costly. The Inquisition, bent on eliminating "subversives," had imprisoned or exiled many of the king's most talented subjects.

To Napoleon, Spain had been simply a poor ally. Charles IV had given him little money, untrustworthy troops, and antiquated warships. Spain had also failed to close Portugal, as instructed, to the British, and was itself violating the Continental System. Finally, in 1806, Godoy had mobilized Spanish armies against "the enemy," then dismissed them after Jena.

Iberia was unprofitable—and dangerous. Neither Spain

[7] For details, see pp. 139ff and 152ff.

nor Portugal had much military strength, but either might allow the British to land troops. Iberia fouled Napoleon's system. And would not the Spanish be grateful if he took over and reformed the country?

INVASION Godoy, on promise of a kingdom in Portugal, allowed French troops to enter Spain peacefully, initially to conquer Portugal (Treaty of Fontainebleau, October 1807).

A French army under General Andoche Junot seized Lisbon in November 1807. The Portuguese royal family was taken to Brazil by the British navy. More French troops invaded Spain, occupied the northern fortresses, and marched on Madrid. At first there was little opposition to the entry of the "allies." By March 1808 there were 100,000 French troops in Spain. Marshal Murat, "Lieutenant of the Emperor," took command. He was exultant, hoping to be made king of Spain. His wife, Caroline Bonaparte, was pressing Napoleon relentlessly in his behalf—to no avail. The emperor had selected Joseph Bonaparte.

EXIT THE BOURBONS The Bourbons made things easy for Napoleon. On March 17, 1808, the crown prince overthrew his father and proclaimed himself Ferdinand VII. He appealed to the French emperor for support. So did Charles IV and Maria Louisa. Napoleon was delighted. Meanwhile Murat, with 40,000 troops, entered Madrid to the wild cheers of the populace; it was assumed he backed Ferdinand.

Napoleon instructed Murat to send all the Bourbons to meet him at Bayonne, just inside France, for "talks."[8] Ferdinand went fearfully; but reasoned that if the emperor opposed him, he was lost anyway. He had less courage, it proved, than his subjects. On May 10, at Bayonne, both kings abdicated and all their possible successors renounced their rights. All were dispatched to palatial imprisonment in France.

[8] Ferdinand offered Godoy—captured at Aranjuez after hiding three days wrapped in a rug—for good measure.

Dos de Mayo At Madrid, however, there had been trouble. On May 2—Dos de Mayo—the capital rose in insurrection. Murat was ready. Napoleon had predicted an uprising, even hoped for one so that the Madrileños could be treated to the "whiff of grapeshot." Murat's troops moved in from the outskirts, driving the people before them. Cannon fired point blank into the crowds, the cavalry following them up.

At the Puerta del Sol, the Mamelukes, fired at from buildings, dismounted and charged inside, killing men, women, and children and rolling their heads into the streets. Spain still remembers. In popular history the *Dos de Mayo* is the day the demon emperor of the French set Moslems on the Christians of Madrid. There were only eighty-seven Mamelukes there, but Napoleon was thenceforth identified by the rebels with the Moors, ancient oppressors of the Spanish.

The rebellion was smashed. Napoleon was pleased. Surely Spanish morale was broken! Madrid, in fact, would not rise again. But Madrid was not Paris; to cow the capital was not so important as in France. The Spanish were province-oriented. The Madrileños—men, women and children—fighting with obsolete weapons, kitchen knives, sticks and stones and heaving furniture, tiles, and chamberpots from upper floors, had set an example all Spain would follow.

Junta of Bayonne Napoleon was further pleased—and misled —by the Spanish National Junta he called to Bayonne. In May 1808 distinguished Spaniards flooded into the little town. The Prince del Castelfranco, the dukes del Parque and d'Infantado came, as did eminent liberals such as Francisco de Cabarrús, Gonzalo O'Farrill, Pedro Cevallos, and Miguel José de Azanza. Two archbishops appeared, and the heads of the Franciscan and Dominican orders. The Cardinal de Bourbon, cousin of Charles IV, sent his best wishes. Gaspar Jovellanos, Spain's most famous liberal author, sent an encouraging letter.

The emperor wrote enthusiastically to Joseph, who was reluctant to leave Naples. Spain was a richer kingdom; the opportunities for reform were unlimited. No war of conquest would be necessary. The notables of Spain had come to greet him; they wanted a new dynasty. On June 7, Joseph arrived at Bayonne. Murat and Caroline were named to succeed him at Naples.

Joseph was welcomed cordially by representatives of the nobility, clergy, army, and towns. The Junta approved a liberal constitution. He was crowned (July 7) by the Archbishop of Burgos. He easily assembled a ministry of eminent Spaniards. In high spirits, he and his cabinet left for Madrid on July 9, escorted by Imperial and Royal (mostly French) Guards.

SPAIN IN REBELLION   Fired initially by the clergy, who saw Napoleon as the devil's servant, a grass-roots rebellion blazed up and spread. Most nobles, fearing loss of their traditional authority, happily took leadership. Those who urged moderation were often lynched. The religious peasants were easy recruits. So were the workers, already violently anti-French, especially in the ports, ruined by the Continental System. Spanish liberals, noble and commoner, had to make a choice between following the popular cause and being *afrancesados*—Francophiles, with "traitor" implied. The majority opted for the rebels, including Jovellanos. But an impressive group, in numbers and talent, stuck with Joseph. (See p. 105.)

Thorough provincials, the people thought of themselves as Catalans, Aragonese, Castilians. They fought not for Spain but for crown and church. Theirs was a medieval nationalism, but nevertheless powerful. They identified Ferdinand VII with the "hero kings" who had freed Spain from the Moors, and because of the 700-year crusade, patriotism and church loyalty were inseparable.

In the provinces not occupied by the French, rebel juntas took over. Armies of volunteers formed around regular regiments. In the north the leaders were the aging General Garcia de la Cuesta, Don José Palafox, and Don Joaquin Blake, the latter two of part Irish ancestry. In the south there were Francisco de Castaños, Count Montijo de Guzmán, the Irish General Felix Jones, and the French émigré Marquis de Coupigny. Later, the armies would prove extremely fragile. In the summer of 1808, however, they could contend with the overconfident French, who had badly overextended themselves.

ENTER AND EXIT JOSEPH   Joseph proceeded easily to Madrid, the road cleared by Marshal Jean Bessières, who set to flight disorganized rebels under Cuesta and Blake at Medina del Rio Seco. But he was alarmed at the greeting "his people" gave him. Cities and villages fell silent at his approach; the inhabitants hid behind boarded doors and windows as he passed. He wrote Napoleon repeatedly, some days several times. The country, he said, was fused to explode. "No one has told Your Majesty the truth." Nonsense, the emperor replied. Courage. "All the better people" are for you.

Joseph found Madrid (on July 20) in sinister quiet. Almost immediately, however, some of his followers began disappearing. A week after his arrival, he learned why. At Bailén, in Andalusia, General Dupont's corps of 30,000 had been captured by Castaños's rebels. Others had forced Marshal Jeannot de Moncey out of Valencia. French commander as well as king, Joseph had to decide whether to stand or withdraw. Rebel victories indicated there might be great hordes marching on the capital. Actually, he had more troops than they.

On July 31, after eleven days in Madrid, he retreated, and in August regrouped all his forces north of the Ebro River. Napoleon was beside himself. "I can see . . . I must return and set the machine in motion again." Joseph was ready to call it quits. He did not want to be a king by conquest, he wrote Napoleon. "I would not live long enough to atone for all that evil." The emperor ignored his plea.

A LESSON FOR THE SPANISH   Napoleon raced to Erfurt (October 1808) to confer with the tsar. Alexander renewed the alliance with France on promise of French mediation in the Russo-Turkish war, begun in 1806. With central Europe "safe," the emperor ordered the Grande Armée from Germany to Spain. Meanwhile in August, Junot had pounced with careless confi-

dence on a British invasion force at Vimeiro and had been defeated by Sir Arthur Wellesley, later the duke of Wellington.
Portugal was lost.

It was Joseph's "defeat," however, that plagued Napoleon.
The nation defied him in Spain. A rebel junta, governing in
the name of Ferdinand VII, occupied Madrid. The Spanish
victory at Bailén inspired France's enemies all over Europe.
Rebel propaganda mockingly spoke of Joseph's "visit." He was
now "Pepe Botellas" (Joe Bottle)—a bungling drunkard.

The emperor meant to teach the Spanish a lesson they
would never forget. In November he had 300,000 men in Spain—
outnumbering the Spanish three to one. In less than a month he
shattered the rebel armies and took Madrid. Unexpectedly, a
British army from Portugal appeared to his rear. Sir John Moore
with 30,000 men! Napoleon gleefully departed to lead the attack on *les Anglais*. But news arrived that Austria was arming.
He sent Marshal Nicolas Soult after Moore, who got his army
aboard ship at Corunna but was killed. The emperor (January
16) left for Paris.

Napoleon gave orders making Joseph commander again
in Spain. Was all not settled? The king had Madrid. The rebel
armies were crushed. Without Moore, Portugal was at the mercy
of the French.

"THAT . . . SPANISH AFFAIR" But Madrid was not important.
The British, more determined than he thought, returned Wellesley (Wellington) to Portugal within weeks. The Spanish armies,
supplied by the British, re-formed and challenged again. For
five years they lost every major battle against the French, but
always reappeared.

To their aid came hordes of guerrillas. The rebel government, which retreated to Seville, then to Cadiz, legalized the
murder of Frenchmen. The mountainous terrain favored the
bands; the people protected and supplied them. Churchmen
blessed them and passed information; some monks became
leaders. A widely used catechism read: "Are we at liberty to kill
the French? Not only are we but it is our sacred duty to do so."

Joseph's dearest wish was to be a Spanish monarch, govern constitutionally, and bring enlightenment and prosperity to his people. But the Spanish and their British allies would give him no peace. Had Napoleon returned to Spain, the war might have been won. But that was not to be. The French always outnumbered the enemy. But Joseph could not coordinate their operations, nor could Napoleon, directing operations from Paris. Spain, save Cadiz, was occupied. But the French could not dislodge Wellington from Portugal. Finally recognized by the Spanish as allied commander in 1812, he emerged from Portugal and drove Joseph from Spain in 1813. Meanwhile the war cost the Empire 300,000 men, a billion francs in specie, and untold amounts in matériel and arms. The Spanish colonies, some of which, at least, Napoleon hoped would declare for Joseph, all refused. (See Chapter 6.) "That miserable Spanish affair," Napoleon would later say, ". . . was what killed me."

Still, Joseph's reign is important in Spanish history, both because of the reforms he attempted and the effect they had in promoting liberalism on the rebel side.

THE AUSTRIAN WAR Napoleon's involvement in Spain encouraged the warhawks at Vienna. They included Count Philipp von Stadion, the chancellor; Maria Ludovica, the beautiful and spirited new empress, third wife of Francis I; the Baron Josef von Hormayr, a prolific propagandist; and, belatedly, the Archduke Charles, Austria's top soldier. A swarm of exiles goaded them on—Prussia's Freidrich von Gentz and Baron vom Stein, Corsica's Pozzo de Borgo, Madame de Staël, and others.

Austria seemed ready. For a nationally polyglot empire considerable spirit had been generated. Volunteers had swelled the Landwehr (reserve) and regular army to 500,000. Moreover, the zealots were convinced that the German states would follow Austria's lead.

In April 1809 the Archduke Charles proclaimed a war of German national liberation and marched into Bavaria with 170,000 men. The Germans, however, did not rally to him. There was a minor uprising in Westphalia, but the kingdom stood firm.[9] The Tyrol, which Austria had ceded to Bavaria in the peace of Pressburg in 1805 (see p. 64), revolted against the Bavarian government. But there it was German versus German until the French gave aid to finish off the valiant Andreas Hofer and his mountaineers.

Prussia was neutral. The other German states backed Napoleon, who crossed the Rhine with 200,000 men in April. In mid-May, he was in Vienna. The Archduke Charles withdrew north of the Danube. His brother, the Archduke John, who had invaded Italy, was prevented by Eugène from coming to his aid. Reenforced by Eugène's army, Napoleon defeated the Archduke Charles at Wagram (July 5–6, 1809). Austria made peace. By the Treaty of Schönbrunn (October 14, 1809), Austria lost territory to Bavaria, Russia, and the Grand Duchy of Warsaw.

THE ILLYRIAN PROVINCES More humiliating, Austria yielded to France what remained of its Balkan lands south of the Save River.[10] These, together with Venetian Istria and Dalmatia (given to Italy in 1805), Ragusa (seized in 1808), and the Ionian Islands (captured by Russia in 1799 and returned to France in 1807), became the Illyrian Provinces.[11] They were declared an integral part of France, and placed under the administration of Marshal Auguste Marmont, who was responsible directly to Napoleon.

GRAND DUCHY OF TUSCANY The Kingdom of Etruria (Tuscany), a Spanish secondogeniture, was dissolved in 1807, and annexed to France in 1808, completing Napoleon's control of north Italy. In 1809 he named Elisa Bonaparte Bacciochi, his eldest sister, Grand Duchess of Tuscany. She had ruled adjacent

[9] A renegade Prussian major, Ferdinand von Schill, and the young duke of Brunswick led invasions of the kingdom. But Jerome's German troops remained loyal. Both were driven out. Schill was trapped and died a hero at Stralsund. Brunswick was rescued by the British navy.

[10] Hungarian Dalmatia, Croatia, Austrian Istria, and the port of Trieste, plus some islands.

[11] Italy was compensated for Istria and Dalmatia with the Southern Tyrol.

Parma-Piacenza since 1805. An intelligent and forceful woman, she governed well.

DEMISE OF THE PAPAL STATES   There had been a long contest of wills between Napoleon and Pius VII. The emperor claimed authority over the pope in all temporal matters. "We return to the time of Charlemagne." Pius defied him, denounced the imperial catechism in 1806, stopped consecrating French bishops in 1807, and refused to appoint more non-Italian cardinals. In 1808 Napoleon had Rome occupied and added the eastern Papal States to Italy.

In June 1809 Napoleon annexed to France the remaining Papal States, including Rome. Pius excommunicated him. The news reached Napoleon when he seemed to be losing the war, his army beaten back, stalled at the Danube. Short of temper, he shouted orders to arrest "that monk." General François de Miollis, in Rome, sent the pontiff off to Savona, where he was held until 1812.[12] How else, Napoleon asked, could one punish a pope "who preaches revolt and civil war?" The reference was to Spain, especially.

The pope, though imprisoned, remained a power in Europe. Meanwhile, however, his states were subjected to vigorous rule by Napoleon's prefects.

THE AUSTRIAN MARRIAGE   If the emperor could have foreseen the future, he would have led his mighty armies, in person, against Wellington and the Spanish. But he was obsessed with strengthening his north European system and perpetuating his dynasty. Marriage to a Habsburg princess, he decided, might accomplish both—by making Austria a "natural" ally and providing a wife who could give him a son. In December 1809 he divorced Josephine and in March 1810 married the eighteen-year-old Archduchess Marie Louise, daughter of the Austrian emperor.

To everyone's surprise, the dynastic marriage turned into

[12] In 1812 he was transferred to Fontainebleau. Forced to sign a new concordat (which he later repudiated), he was allowed to return to Rome in 1814.

a love match. The buxom Marie Louise, at first terrified of Napoleon, gave herself to him fully. Her forty-year-old husband, the lean soldier and perpetual traveler, became a homebody. He grew fat and sedentary. His happiness influenced him to send Masséna, then Marmont, to Spain to fight *les Anglais,* when his presence there could have been decisive. After the birth of his son (March 1811), the emperor was even more tied to Paris, though preparing for war with Russia.

CENTRALIZATION OF CONTROL Nevertheless, Napoleon continued to centralize control of Europe. In February 1810, before he was married, Napoleon proclaimed his prospective son "King of Rome," and Rome the second capital of the Empire. Eugène, who had expected to become king of Italy, found his term as viceroy limited to 20 years, after which Italy would fall to the King of Rome (or a second son).[13] Murat rightly feared that Naples was in jeopardy as well.

Louis Bonaparte, in June 1810, found his country occupied by French troops and French officials enforcing the Continental System. On July 1 he abdicated and fled into exile in Austria. Holland was annexed to France. Napoleon also annexed in 1810 the Hanse cities—Hamburg, Bremen, and Lübeck—northern Hanover, part of Westphalia, and other minor principalities, including Oldenburg, ruled by a relative of the tsar.

In Spain, during 1810, Joseph was relegated to Madrid, and most of the country put under generals responsible to Paris. Napoleon took over direction of the war—from Paris. Until 1812 Joseph was king in name only.

At the end of 1810, however, the tsar renounced the Continental System, and the French alliance was broken. Napoleon began preparing for war, and conciliated the satellite rulers. As we shall discuss in the conclusion, however, Napoleon had further plans for centralizing his power—after he won the war with Russia.

---

[13] Eugène was compensated with the Grand Duchy of Frankfurt and promised a principality in Italy or elsewhere.

THE GRAND EMPIRE   In early 1812 Napoleon dominated Europe as had no ruler since Roman times. France was almost twice the size it had been in 1789. Beyond stood the satellite kingdoms of Italy, Naples, Spain, and Westphalia. Allied with France were the States of the Confederation of the Rhine, including the Grand Duchies of Warsaw and Berg, the Swiss Confederation,[14] Denmark, Norway, Prussia, and Austria.

Napoleon marched on Russia with a truly European army. Of the 600,000 only 200,000 were from the original 83 French departments, another 100,000 were from new departments, 300,000 were foreign — German, Austrian, Polish, Italian, Neapolitan, and others. Joseph commanded more Frenchmen in Spain than Napoleon in Russia.

WEAKNESSES   Despite the formidable extent of the Empire and the irresistible appearance of its army — the largest Europe had ever seen, three times the size of Russia's apparent forces — it had weaknesses.

The Spanish war had steadily sapped French strength and morale. Moreover, the rebels' stubborn resistance had "awakened" other European nationalities, even in the "solid" satellite kingdoms. The Prussians marched under obvious duress; the Austrians were not firmly attached to France by the imperial marriage. Anti-French sentiment had been increased by heavy war taxes, levies of food, equipment, and heavier conscription quotas.

In addition, the Continental System had not succeeded fully as a weapon and had been drastically modified. Napoleon had begun by allowing French grain to be exported to Britain in 1809 so that the peasants could pay his taxes. He shortly lifted restrictions on other exports — foodstuffs and manufactures. In January 1810 he legalized the sale of prize cargos, British goods, at 40 percent tariff. In July 1810 he authorized licenses for the importation of "contraband" on payment of 50 percent tariffs.

---

[14] Formerly the Helvetic Republic.

STRENGTHS Napoleon, nevertheless, was not displeased with the Continental System. It had promoted industry in Europe. It had been partially responsible for a severe recession in Britain during 1810–1812. He intended to force Russia and its ally, Sweden, to rejoin the System. His chances seemed good. Russia was not the power it later became. Its population was less than that of Napoleonic France, its government primitive, and its industry almost nil. Sweden was a very minor power. Moreover, the emperor had helped foment a war between the United States and Britain by negating the Continental System (1811) for the Americans (see Chapter 6).

Rationally, Napoleon had many reasons to be optimistic in 1812. But his enemies would most irrationally oppose him — and win.

CHAPTER FIVE

The Enlightened Proconsuls

"THE PEOPLES of Germany, those of France, Italy, of Spain desire equality and want liberal ideas [applied] . . ." wrote Napoleon to Jerome. This was one of his major misconceptions. In the short run, most peoples did not fully understand the benefits of "revolution," and were often hostile to change—least in Italy; most in Spain. In the long run, however, Napoleon's objectives were understood, and his greatness is more fully appreciated today because he did try, consciously, to modernize every country he dominated. It would be idiotic, of course, to say that the emperor acted purely on principle. His benefits were intended also to win the peoples away from their traditional leaders. More efficient institutions were introduced to make the nations more useful to the Empire.

ITALY   Eugène de Beauharnais was twenty-three when he became viceroy of the Kingdom of Italy (May 1805). Athletic, self-
assured, he had his father's aristocratic features and Josephine's
dark coloration. A soldier for almost ten years, veteran of three
wars, Eugène was mature beyond his years. Still, at first, he was
ordered to make no major decision without consulting Napoleon—"Even if the moon is falling on Milan. . . ." The emperor's confidence in Eugène's ability to govern, however, was
soon absolute. It was the same with war. In 1805 Napoleon let
Masséna command Eugène's army. In 1809 Eugène led it himself,
and by his victories set the stage for Napoleon's triumph at
Wagram (see p. 77).

In 1806, meanwhile, Eugène married Augusta of Bavaria,
whose father Napoleon had made a king. A dark-haired sylph
of seventeen, she was a fairy-tale princess—beautiful, good—
and yet spirited enough to upbraid Napoleon for not respecting
love. The marriage, however, was happy. She gave Eugène seven
children, and the court at Milan had for some an oppressively
homey atmosphere. Eugène was a model ruler, loyal to Napoleon to the end; his wife, though she thought the emperor did
not properly reward him, stood by him always.

Eugène's constitution was that of the Italian Republic,
amended to include monarchal forms. Napoleon was the executive; Eugène his deputy. The viceroy ruled with a ministry and
a *consulta* of prominent citizens. Laws were framed by a council
of state assisted by young auditors.

The legislature, in the beginning, was a one-house body of
75 men elected, indirectly, by universal manhood suffrage. Had
it so remained—despite property qualifications for electors—
the government would have been more democratic than that of
France. The legislature, however, debated incessantly and
accomplished little. On Napleon's order, Eugène dismissed it
after its first session (1805) and never called it again, though it
was not abolished.

A Senate, provided by constitutional amendment, assumed
the legislative function. Appointed by Eugène, it comprised
some seventy members—two from each department, the min-

Eugène de Beauharnais, viceroy of Italy. Son of Josephine by her first marriage to Viscount Alexandre de Beauharnais, he was Napoleon's most effective royal proconsul and a superb military commander. *(The New York Public Library)*

isters and grand officers of state, and a number of judges. According to Napoleon's view, reform had first priority. Viceroy and Senate could act quickly. Later, perhaps, Italy could afford more popular government.

With few exceptions, Italians, including the intelligentsia, accepted his view. They merely compared Eugène's government with previous ones, and found it better. The viceroy himself, if not popular, was widely respected.

As to rights, there was full roster, carried over from the constitution of the Republic—essentially those enumerated in the French Declaration of the Rights of Man. The constitution also declared the abolition of feudalism, guilds, and the feudal rights of the church. The Code Napoléon was introduced in January 1806.

For administration, Italy had 24 departments under prefects *(prefetti)* appointed by the viceroy; the departments were divided into districts, cantons, and municipalities. The courts were reformed, also following the French pattern, with a court of cassation at the top and justices of the peace at the bottom.

In Italy, as in France, there was a conscious effort to promote social change—to create an amalgam of leadership. The old nobles were allowed to keep their titles. Some were given offices—for example, Count Caprara. New nobles were appointed, however, for their services. Melzi d'Eril, the former vice-president of Italy, was made a duke. The middle class was initially led by people like Giovanni Paradisi, Ferdinando Marescalchi, and Giuseppe Prina, all of whom, however, later became counts, making room for new men.

Napoleon was vitally interested in the new generation. "Surround yourself . . . with young men" he wrote Eugène. "The old ones are good for nothing." He saw the army, especially, as an instrument for changing society and reducing provincialism. "My object," he told Eugène, "is to effect a cultural revolution. . . ." The officers' schools were open to men of all provinces and classes, though few peasants or workers were educationally qualified. All lived and trained together as equals, and had to use the same Italian dialect, Tuscan. It was the language of Florence (outside the kingdom) and of the Italian Renaissance, thus, to Napoleon, "pure" Italian. Elitism—of talent—was practiced. Those selected for the Royal Guard had special schools. They developed fierce *esprit de corps* which infected the whole army. Promotion was based on performance; class distinctions were eroded.

Among the satellite armies the Italian ranked only second to the Westphalian, which was built around Hessian regiments with long military tradition. Not all the officers or men were Napoleonists, or even pro-French. But most were opposed to the return of the Old Regime. This can be said as well of Eugène's judges and bureaucrats.

For civilians, the College of Auditors, the administration, and the courts served as training grounds in efficient methods and procedures. The tendency was for aristocrats to choose the courts, and the sons of the middle class the administration. Together, however, they formed a new breed of civil servants. It was these men, with former officers of Eugène's army, who led revolutions later in the nineteenth century.

The church functioned under a concordat of 1803, which the pope had called "Jacobin" and never ratified, but did not renounce. The Italian church accepted it. The viceroy put the church under civil control, but made a bishop his minister of "cults." Except for minor disturbances in 1809, when Pius VII was arrested, the church cooperated well. It operated the primary schools, issued royal proclamations from the pulpit, and the like. It accepted, without much commotion, the confiscation of the property of monastic orders.

Laissez-faire principles were the rule in Italy. But the government was not idle. Internal tariffs were eliminated. An extensive road system was constructed; waterways were improved. Napoleon adjusted tariffs to encourage the production of raw materials and food for France and the purchase of French manufactures by Italy. Nevertheless, domestic industry as well as agriculture prospered. Manufacturers converted to rough cloth for the domestic market and crepes, sheer fabrics, and other Italian specialties to meet French demands, as well as expanded Austrian, Russian, and Middle Eastern markets.

In the process Italian production switched from the

putting-out system to factory operation. In 1812 one plant at Vicenza employed 6000 people. By 1814 Bologna had 500 factories, Modena 400. The manufacturing of wool and cotton cloth had expanded. All this was done while giving Napoleon what he wanted—raw silk, some cotton, grain, meat animals, oranges, lemons, and so on. The value of silk exported in 1812 was 80 million lire, 40 percent higher than in 1805.[1] The economy suffered an initial shock from the Continental System, but adjusted rapidly, taking advantage of markets lost to the British and increasing overland trade with the Middle East. It hurt less after 1810, when Napoleon's licensing system was implemented.

Italians also became master smugglers. The island of Vis, in the Adriatic, was notorious as a depot for contraband. Eugène's navy destroyed the base in 1810, but it revived. Cotton, sugar, coffee, tobacco, chocolate, and other colonial products came from Vis, the ports of the Balkans, Greece, and even the French Ionian Islands. But the principal warehouses were on Malta, which became valuable to the British beyond their wildest dreams.

The minister of finances was Giuseppe Prina, who balanced the budget and kept it in balance until 1813. This he did without burdening the people greatly. His mainstay was the capitation tax, on heads of families. It ran an average of 176 lire—about 134 francs. Other revenues were raised through indirect taxes and the sale of confiscated property. Overall, taxes in Italy were about one-third less than in France.

Dour, businesslike, a human computer forever checking accounts, Prina was totally absorbed in his work. Efficient and incorruptible, he set high standards for his subordinates. Graft —a time-honored "sport" in Italy—was punished viciously. Italians owed much to Prina, but hated him. Who loves a tax collector?

It was Prina also who managed the confiscated "National" properties—largely taken from the monasteries—worth about 500 million lire (400 million francs). By careful control of sales and of paper issued against the properties, the kingdom netted

[1] Lire = .76 francs.

some 70 percent of their assessed value—a much better return than any other government, including France, got from similar holdings.

Italy's Ministry of Waterways and Roads (Acque e Strade) under Giovanni Paradisi greatly improved communications. Roads ran from Adriatic ports to the passes through the Alps to France or to the Po River and from its ports to the passes. Among cooperative French-Italian projects were new routes over the Mont Cenis and Simplon passes to France, and between Venice and Trieste (in Illyria). Along the beautiful Riviera coast, the famous Corniche was cut into the cliffs that abut the sea. (The roadbed is still in use.) This also carried goods from the Italian departments of France, from Naples and Lucca-Piombino. The arrangement of routes, all leading to France— those from Naples mostly bypassing Italy—betrays the fact that Napoleon did not favor economic unification of the peninsula. It might promote pan-Italian nationalism. He felt he could use and control Italian and Neapolitan nationalism, but feared a more far-reaching variety.

Paradisi also directed public works, including the beautification of Milan. The cathedral, second in size only to St. Peter's in Rome, got a new facade. Arches were built at the gates of the city, the most famous the Porta Ticinese. The La Scala Opera house was remodeled. At Monza the palace of the Lombard kings was refurbished.

With his finances in good order and many convinced progressives to assist him, Eugène mounted public welfare and education programs which rivaled those of France. He created a National Council for Public Hygiene responsible for public health and sanitation. It enforced vaccination for smallpox, examined water and sewer systems, and supervised epidemic control. The council's advice guided the administration of hospitals, homes for orphans, the aged, and the indigent, and public works where health was involved. The church continued to provide staffs for institutions, but under public supervision.

The minister of education was Giovanni Scopoli, a rare combination of scholar and administrator. The control of all the schools was centralized, including the universities at Bologna, Pavia, and Padua. The work of professors and researchers was subsidized. Attached to the universities, though they seldom taught, were literary lights such as Vincenzo Monti and Ugo Foscolo. Pavia boasted Alessandro Volta, after whom the electrical unit of force is named.

Lycées (high schools) were organized in each department. There was, in addition, a *collège* for women in Milan. This had no equivalent in France. The lower schools were run by the church. A special school, modeled after the École Polytechnique, trained engineers.

A Royal Institute was founded, with branches in all the major cities. Eugène patronized the theaters and opera, which were put under central direction. He also sponsored a conservatory of music and an academy of fine arts. The halls of the latter were often graced by the Italian Antonio Canova, the most renowned sculptor of his day.

The handsome and willful Canova declined Napoleon's invitation to live at the Imperial Court, but he made numerous statues and busts of the Bonapartes. His most famous is the reclining nude of Pauline, for which she posed. ("The studio was well heated.")[2] More representative of his art, which began a classical revival, is the *Cupid and Psyche,* in the Louvre, and works on mythical themes held by museums in Rome, Naples, London, Munich, Berlin, and elsewhere.

One essential ingredient, however, was missing from intellectual life—freedom. Censorship was not severe—Vincenzo Cuoco, one of the fathers of Italian unification, published a newspaper in Milan—but it was applied. There was little to bother about, however, except subtle anti-Napoleonic propaganda—for example, in classical plays denouncing tyranny. The propaganda of secret nationalist societies surfaced only in the latter years.

Generally, the intelligentsia supported Napoleon and Eugène, voluntarily glorifying the regime. There is a ring of sincerity especially in their earlier work—the poetry of Vin-

[2] The most shocking to Napoleon was a nude of himself—for which he did not pose. It went into the cellars of the Louvre. Lord Wellington bought it in 1815, and it may be seen today in Apsley House, London.

cenzo Monti, for example. Cuoco "fled" to Naples—where the pan-national movement was stronger—and was patronized by Joseph and Murat. Other notables stayed put. After the loss of 20,000 Italians in Russia there was some open hostility to Napoleon, not so much to Eugène. But in 1813–1814, when intellectuals saw their choice was between the return of the Old Regime and the Napoleonic system, most chose the latter, or remained silent. Ugo Foscolo, poet, novelist, and no longer young, insisted on joining Eugène's army to fight the Austrians.

Eugène's was a model kingdom. So solidly based was it that its army was still fighting the Austrians—and Murat, who became a turncoat—when Napoleon abdicated in 1814. Had the people been allowed to vote, it is more than probable that Eugène would have retained his throne. It is not strange that northern Italy became the principal locus of revolutionary activity in the nineteenth century.

NAPLES Napoleon seized Naples in 1806 to deny its ports to the British and improve the French position in the Mediterranean. With Joseph in Naples, Spain his ally, and the Ottoman empire at war with Britain and Russia,[3] he hoped to ruin British trade, and perhaps in time achieve naval superiority in the Mediterranean. He expected little profit from Naples itself.

Naples was economically backward; its society feudal. Its land was held mostly by owners of gigantic *latifundia,* the crown, and the church. Most peasants, in effect, were serfs. Poverty was extreme, starvation common, banditry rife (in Calabria, banditry was a profession, sons following their fathers). Ignorance was incredible. Agricultural methods were medieval (wooden plows, no fertilizer), and diseases such as malaria and tuberculosis were endemic. The people had a sleepy character but were prone to outbursts of inhuman brutality. The conditions of life were well reflected in the churches, where the statues and paintings ran to scenes of martydom, with contorted figures dripping blood. It was an agricultural country with a

[3] Under French encouragement Turkey declared war on both in 1806. It made peace with Britain in 1809, but not with Russia until 1812.

very small middle class. Investment capital was scarce. Industry was a small factor in the economy. There was very little national or even provincial spirit, except perhaps among the *lazzaroni* of the capital, who took pride in being the slickest thieves in Christendom.

Joseph Bonaparte, styled Giuseppe Napoleone (Joseph Napoleon), ruled Naples from 1806 until mid-1808, when he went to Spain.[4] The most likable of the Bonapartes, at thirty-eight still slender and handsome, he was kingly in appearance and polished, yet democratic, in manner. As thoroughly devoted to reform as Napoleon, he was a more sincere believer in popular constitutional government. It was his plans that guided Neapolitan domestic policy until the fall of the kingdom.

Murat (Gioacchino Napoleone) and Caroline Bonaparte, who succeeded Joseph, were less reform-minded, but carried on most of his projects. The vain Gascon, with his shock of curly, black hair, bizarre uniforms, and jewel-studded trappings, was a king after the hearts of the *lazzaroni*. He was a creature of war, however, who, in civil affairs, depended heavily on his ministers. Caroline, pretty if overly busty, had more political talent and a Machiavellian deviousness that even Talleyrand, one of her numerous lovers, envied. Her chief objective in life was to retain the crown for herself and her children—with or without Murat.[5] She wielded power by posing as Napoleon's defender against her increasingly nationalist husband. As the emperor's star faded, however, she became Neapolitan herself, and pushed Murat—his soldier's conscience so torn that he wept —into joining the Allies (1814) to save their throne. It bought them only one troubled year.

Joseph took a positive approach to reform. He abolished feudalism as soon as the conquest was over. When his council of state debated too long over details of his decree, he lost his temper. "The people have groaned too long under . . . abuses; they shall be freed, and if obstacles appear, never doubt,

---

[4] His queen, née Julie Clary, remained in France with their two daughters, though she did visit Naples briefly at the end of the reign. She never joined him in Spain.
[5] Two boys and a girl. Achille, the eldest, became a prominent resident of Florida in the 1820s and is buried in Tallahassee.

Joseph Bonaparte, Napoleon's elder brother, king of Naples, later
Spain. Handsome, articulate, socially adept, a novelist, *philosophe*,
and inveterate "do-gooder," he was a successful enlightened monarch
in Naples, but he failed in Spain, where a soldier-king was required.
(The New York Public Library)

I will . . . smash them." Nevertheless, his program called for gradual elimination of feudalism, and he delayed action on the Code Napoléon and other matters. He had plans to restructure society, the economy, the administration and courts, and much more. But he elected to move slowly so as not to alienate the only educated people in Naples—the nobility and the high middle class. He wanted maximum native participation in the government.

In the beginning, however, his six key ministers included three Frenchmen—Miot de Melito (Interior), Pierre Louis Roederer (Finance), and Christophe Saliceti[6] (Police and War). The Neapolitans were Michelangelo Cianciulli (Justice), Prince Pignatelli-Cerchiara (Marine), and the Marquis de Gallo (Foreign Affairs). The reformers were Miot, Roederer, and Cianciulli. The council of state, however, which drafted laws, was overwhelmingly Neapolitan.

As a step toward greater democracy, Joseph instituted limited popular government at the local level. The existing fourteen provinces were divided into districts, "governments" (voting areas only), and municipalities. The king appointed provincial intendants, subintendants, mayors, and their councils. He made his selections, however, from lists drawn by the voters, who included all male adults who paid a minimum tax.[7] It was a modest beginning, but at least Neapolitans began developing voting experience.

The king abolished feudal and church courts (1806). Cianciulli was charged with transferring cases to existing royal courts and planning a new judicial system. Meanwhile the judges were instructed to apply the principles of equal justice and equal penalties. French style courts went into operation in 1808, a court of cassation at the top, justices of the peace in the cities and villages, with intermediate civil and criminal courts.

In the interim, the judiciary had been radically restructured to oust reactionaries and install more liberal judges. Finesse had been applied, however; most of those retired had been given awards and shifted to ceremonial offices.

[6] The cadaverous, sinister, former patron of the Bonapartes.
[7] The amount varied with the location, but averaged about 24 ducats ($22) a year.

All the while, the Code Napoléon and French penal code, in careful translation, were circulated by Cianciulli's ministry with interpretive tracts and other aids. Just before his departure in May 1808 Joseph ordered the penal code into effect immediately and the Code Napoléon as of November 1, 1809.

After investigating the monastic orders—one man in ten was a monk—Joseph abolished all but the Franciscans, whom he judged useful. Their wealth—value, 30 million ducats, together with seven times more in crown lands, 200 million—became the national properties.[8] Plans called for maximum distribution to the peasants.

Joseph's program for eliminating feudalism (1806) was gradual but effective. Proprietors lost, without compensation, all personal, juridical, and prohibatory rights. The last-mentioned rights had allowed them to ban certain crops, building, and new methods. Money rights (dues) were to be compensated for by the government—not the peasants. Water courses were freed, and common lands, pastures, and forests ordered divided among users. Murat continued the plan so that by 1811 feudalism was dead.

To encourage landownership, Joseph offered low-interest loans to the peasants. The national properties were made available for purchase by their cultivators. Noble lands were in a different category. Their owners did not have to sell to tenants, but were encouraged to do so by the king and more forcibly, perhaps, by the end of feudalism, which reduced their incomes, and later, by the abolition of entail.[9] In addition, land reclaimed from swamps and marshes and wasteland improved by new methods were offered the peasants. Here rent was low, and 95 percent of the rent paid in the first five years was applied to the purchase price. All too few took advantage of these opportunities.

Joseph also imported French experts to teach new farming techniques to the peasants; they were slow to respond, however.

---

[8] Ducat = 4.45 francs.
[9] Entailed estates could not be sold, but had to be passed down to heirs, thereby perpetuating large holdings.

Suspicious of foreigners, they clung to tradition. The greatest progress was made in introducing new crops, especially cotton. By 1809 Naples could supply two-thirds of the needs of the Empire. Both sugar beets and sugar cane were grown.

Products were difficult to get to market, however. Roads were lacking, partly because Neapolitans had always depended on the seaways, now under British control. Many new roads were constructed or rebuilt—from Naples to Rome, from Naples to Reggio, and from Naples to Brindisi. The king used all available resources, including the manpower of idle French troops. The improvements helped, but commerce still moved slowly.

Roederer consolidated all banks into one, reworked the revenue system, and funded the debt. On the surface, his efforts did not seem crashingly successful. The projected deficit for 1808, when Murat took over, was almost 8 million ducats in a budget of 15 million. But he had paid one-half of the national debt—a total of 100 million ducats—by use of the national properties, and was liquidating the rest. Twenty-three taxes of the Old Regime had been replaced by one tax on land and industry, though other indirect taxes remained. He had also begun the systematic repurchase of feudal rights and those of tax farmers. Murat's minister, Agar de Mosbourg, continued Roederer's policies.

Miot organized a ministry of interior, new to Naples, which supervised general administration, public works, welfare, and more. His greatest success was establishing a system of public schools, which Joseph considered the key to all future progress. Communities financed primary schools, and the royal government *lycées* (high schools). Of 2520 public schools planned, 1500 were operating by the end of Joseph's two-year stay. He also took steps to modernize the once famous university at Salerno.

Joseph founded a royal art museum by consolidating former monastic holdings and adding works from the royal collections. The French artist J. B. Wicar organized a School of Art and Design. Existing schools of music were consolidated and strengthened. The preservation of ruins and antiquities also became a government project. Joseph found that diggings at Pompeii, especially, were being looted for profit. He put a stop to it. Governments since have followed his lead. But for his action, Pompeii would not be the attraction it is today.

Although Joseph was a gradualist, his accomplishments were real. He had charted a course toward modernization for Naples. Decades later, Camillo di Cavour (the "unifier" of Italy) wrote in praise of his work. He regretted only that it had not been followed up after 1815.

Joseph promulgated a constitution on his departure, but Murat refused to recognize it. Instead he promised a more liberal and truly Neapolitan one, which he never delivered. He retained the governmental organization, but replaced all the ministers but Gallo (Foreign Affairs).[10]

Murat's top men were Imperial Councillor of State Daure (Police), Agar de Mosbourg (Finance), Giuseppe Zurlo (Interior), and Francesco Ricciardi (Justice)—two Frenchmen, two Neapolitans. Daure was Napoleon's spy, and while she needed him, Caroline's; she became his mistress. Murat came to depend on Antonio Maghella, Police Prefect of Naples (city) for information. He encouraged Murat's nationalism, as did Zurlo and Ricciardi. Agar was the king's man, even in treason (1813–1814). By 1815 Maghella had led them all into the pan-Italian independence movement. Until the latter days of the regime, however, the nationalists kept their ambitions secret—better than did the king.

Murat instituted the Code Napoléon in 1810. It was never fully enforced, however, and as to civil marriage and divorce, not at all.

Giuseppe Zurlo, meanwhile, carried forward the abolition of feudalism. With the aid of royal commissions, which settled over 8000 cases regarding compensation and the division of commons, the process was completed by late 1810. Benefits to the peasants were obscured by the assumption of some noble rights by municipalities—over waterways and mills, for example —new taxes, which, if lower, were harder to avoid, and conscription. Murat doubled Joseph's rate. Nevertheless feudalism was gone.

---

[10] Saliceti died, perhaps poisoned, in 1809; the others were given new offices.

Zurlo neglected education; the number of public schools declined. He strengthened provincial administration, however, and pushed ahead public works and economic projects. These slowly began to bear fruit. Commerce was fostered by the virtual elimination of banditry, which Murat smashed by massive use of troops and police. The king also ignored the Continental System freely and quickly bid for licenses in 1810. Olive oil, a major product unshippable in quantity except by sea, began to move to market, along with grain and other commodities long stockpiled. Fortunes were made, and prosperity trickled down even to the peasantry. This added to Murat's popularity as well as to his revenues.

Agar, angry over the 1808 deficit, nevertheless followed Roederer's program religiously. In 1809 his budget almost balanced, and in 1810 and 1811 he had surpluses. By 1811 he had liquidated all but 20 million ducats of the national debt. After 1811 Murat's increased military expenses upset the books. Taxes had to be increased, but not so much as to alienate the population.

Joseph had begun building a Neapolitan army, largely to increase national pride. "I want . . . to revive the glory of the name Italian," he wrote Napoleon. The emperor had no faith in Neapolitan troops, who excelled only in deserting, but he let him try. Joseph did reform the Royal Military Academy and founded artillery and polytechnic schools, which gave some nonnobles a chance to rise in status. But he left Murat fewer than 3000 men, disregarding French and foreign units.

Murat wanted an army to bolster his pride and make him independent of Napoleon. He began building in 1808. After the emperor's marriage to the Archduchess Marie Louise he worked harder, fearful that Naples would be integrated into France.[11] In 1810 he had 40,000 troops; by 1812, 80,000. His growing army made him bold. He allowed the official *Monitore* to voice nationalist sentiments, associated with the Freemasons and nascent

[11] Another possibility was that Napoleon would restore the Bourbons. Marie Louise was the granddaughter of Marie Caroline of the Two Sicilies. Murat worried more over this after the summer of 1810, when Napoleon deliberately sabotaged his attempt to invade Sicily.

Carbonari—in Naples, nationalists—and adopted a new flag to replace the French tricolor. Napoleon countered in 1811 by removing French troops, a separate army, from Murat's command—an implied threat to turn them against the king. Murat expressed shock and swore loyalty. "Sire . . . give me your love. I will always be the first grenadier of the Emperor!" He purged his government of nationalists, and was forgiven. In 1812 he was called to the Grande Armée, and went happily.

Murat returned disillusioned, however. His army was still intact; Napoleon had taken only his Guard of 7000. He recalled his old ministers and in 1813—officially 1814—betrayed the emperor. (See pp. 160–161.)

TUSCANY Tuscany had been put at Napoleon's disposal at Lunéville (1801) and converted into a Spanish secundogeniture, the Kingdom of Etruria, in return for nearby Parma and Piacenza, and Louisiana.

The kingdom was not a success. The king died (1803) leaving a minor heir. The queen-regent, a Spanish Bourbon, was weak and unpopular. The state debt mounted to 100 million francs. Leghorn (Livorno) remained an unofficial entrepôt for British goods. Royalist and Jacobin exiles congregated at Florence. At Tilsit (1807) Napoleon decided to remove "that deformity." By the same treaty which doomed Spain (Fontainebleau, October 1807), Prince Manuel Godoy gave up Etruria.[12] Spanish troops withdrew. A French army moved in, burned British goods at Leghorn, and occupied Florence.

In 1808 Tuscany was annexed to France and organized into four departments by Imperial Councillor of State Count Dauchy, who governed initially with a junta of Frenchmen and Italians, including General Menou, a talented eccentric who had become a Moslem in Egypt, and Cesare Balbo, litterateur and historian. In 1809 Napoleon pleased the natives by creating the Grand Duchy of Tuscany—technically part of France but ruled by Elisa Bonaparte Bacciochi.

Elisa, thirty-two, Napoleon's eldest sister, was handsome,

---

[12] Whose queen, like Godoy, was promised a kingdom in Portugal.

Elisa Bonaparte Bacciochi, grand duchess of Tuscany. Napoleon's eldest sister, and very like him in character, she gave her duchy firm and enlightened government. *(The New York Public Library)*

regal in carriage, with strong, regular features and wide-set blue eyes which reflected rare intelligence and steady self-assurance. Educated on a royal scholarship at Saint-Cyr, under the Old Regime *the* school for young ladies, she had a polish her sisters lacked. Married in 1797 to a Corsican captain, Felice Bacciochi, she was a good wife and mother to her two children—a girl and a boy. Unlike the voluptuous Pauline, who courted scandal, her passion was for government, the arts, and literature. "We were never very close, our characters opposed," the emperor said in 1820. In truth, she was very much like him.

Elisa had proved herself as Princess of Lucca-Piombino, granted to her and Prince Bacciochi in 1805. She ruled; her husband commanded their tiny army. Napoleon had been pleased with her administration. She had abolished feudalism, applied the Code Napoléon, liquidated monastic property, and financed new schools and public works. She retained title to her principality, which was not annexed to France.

As Grand Duchess of Tuscany, however, she transferred her court to Florence. Her husband again confined himself to the military. Elisa's chief subordinates were Baron Joseph Gerando and Cesare Balbo. She had full authority over all matters—legal, administrative, and military—subject to Napoleon's approval. He seldom interfered, however, because she usually anticipated his wishes—and made the Grand Duchy financially independent. Moreover, by utilizing the property of the monasteries, she even paid the huge debt incurred by the preceding government.

One of Elisa's first acts was to repeal the double tax on wine—a very popular move. She then introduced equality of taxation, easing the burden of the lower classes, abolished feudalism, and instituted the Code Napoléon. At the same time, however, she introduced conscription, to which the Tuscans responded with wholesale evasion and desertion. She refused to compromise, however, and eventually had the army of 10,000 the emperor demanded. The Tuscans, nevertheless, she wrote Napoleon, were "different from their ancestors." Doubtless she was thinking of the original Buonapartes.

Elisa quickly came to terms with the clergy, who were

powerful and proud—Tuscany had produced many popes—
showing herself a dutiful Catholic in public, but willing to use
imperial power in private. She dissolved the monastic orders,
but pensioned members without prospects and provided homes
for the elderly. The church was placed under civil control, but
she was careful to see that bishops had places of honor at all
ceremonies. The churchmen gave their Grand Duchess no difficulty.

Elisa's court outshone that of Italy and had a legitimate
atmosphere which was lacking in the circles of the flamboyant
Murat in Naples. She favored the French protocol of the Old
Regime and presided with great dignity. This struck a respon-
dent note among the Florentine nobility and pleased the swarm
of artists, writers, and scientists such as Eusebio Valli—a precursor of Pasteur—whose work she rewarded.

The Grand Duchess took great interest in the Academy of
Florence, particularly the section for literature and language.
This was the ancient Academy of Crusca, which she restored to
autonomy, lending her prestige to its major project, a new
Italian dictionary. The Academy's *Vocabulario,* when completed (1811), was circulated throughout the peninsula. This
can be seen as Napoleon's one willful act to foster Italian unity.

She had to order censorship of the works of Vittorio Alfieri, the great poet and apostle of freedom (d. 1803). But she
pressed and cajoled the clergy into giving him a Christian bur-
ial, previously denied, and financed a tomb, designed by Antonio Canova, in the church of Santa Croce. There he rests with
other great Florentines such as Machiavelli and Michelangelo.[13]

The Florentine theater, under state sponsorship, was very
active, though weighted with French classics. For the opera
Elisa cultivated native talent and drew artists from La Scala,
in Milan, and musicians from Naples. Monti, Foscolo, and
other literary lights graced her court. Florence retained its
time-honored place in the artistic and literary life of Italy, if
partly on borrowed talent; but it had always been so.

[13] She also quietly allowed Alfieri's mistress, the duchess of Albany, the "last
Stuart Queen", to live on in Florence.

Like all Napoleon's proconsuls, Elisa left monuments to her reign. These were particularly evident along the street of Dei Calzaioli, which was straightened and widened; the facades of public buildings along the route were restored by the most skilled workmen available. Santa Croce was much beautified.

By creating a French-trained administrative and judicial corps, Elisa also made a contribution to the future of Italy. Pro-Austrian sentiment remained stronger in Tuscany than elsewhere. The government had been quite enlightened. But she left behind many future revolutionaries. Cesare Balbo, her minister, after 1815 in the service of Piedmont, became a leader of the *risorgimento*. Vittorio Alfieri, whom she enshrined, was an inspiration to the Italian nationalists of the nineteenth century.

ROME Before Pius VII was whisked away to Savona (July 1809), General Miollis, assisted by an appointed council of French and Italians, began reforms. In June 1809 the Roman courts were all dissolved, including the tribunals of the Apostolic Chamber. All feudal rights were eliminated in July 1809. At the same time the Code Napoléon and the French commercial code were instituted. In February 1810 the territory was divided into two departments, the Trasimeno, under Antione Roederer,[14] and Rome, under Camille de Tournon. The prefects, however, relied on the backing of French troops, and General François de Miollis retained overall supervision.

The *senatus consultum* (February 1810) which named Rome the second city of the Empire also designated the imprisoned pope chaplain of the emperor and granted him an income and palaces in both cities. But he had to take an oath to the emperor. Pius refused all, and still declined even to consecrate French bishops. His life at Savona was made less comfortable and for a time even his writing materials were taken away, but to no avail.

The pope, moreover, managed to create difficulties in Rome. During 1810 Miollis dissolved most of the monastic orders and confiscated their property. Pius, however, forbade

---

[14] Son of Pierre Louis Roederer.

the purchase of the properties, which drastically thinned the ranks of buyers. He similarly forbade the clergy to take an oath of loyalty to the emperor. The majority obeyed. Miollis tried to compromise on the wording, but got nowhere, and had to resort to deporting nonjuring clergy. The oath was soon extended to lawyers and booksellers, many of whom also refused it, though they faced loss of property as well as exile.

Rome was extremely difficult to govern. Oddly, the French found the nobles to be most trustworthy as officials. The middle class, contrary to expectations, did not welcome the secularization of society. Almost all, from artisans to lawyers, had built their success by serving the Holy See. Most of the common people were emotionally attached to the Papacy, and whatever benefits they received from the French were offset by regular taxes and the draft. Conscription proved almost totally ineffective. Response to the first call (1810) proved typical. Irate mothers demonstrated in Rome. Most of the draftees—only 450—deserted. The Code Napoléon was never enforced, nor the courts and administration fully reformed.

The French governors had successes, nevertheless. Religious liberty was protected. Notably, the Jews were freed from the ghetto and granted full civil rights. The French tax system was introduced. Monopolies held by the state or nobles on items such as tobacco, liquor, and cards, were abolished. Camille de Tournon did notable work in the reorganization of hospitals and prisons.

Both Tournon and Roederer sponsored experimentation with new crops. Cotton growing proved very successful. A new manufacturing plant for cotton cloth was put in operation. Raw cotton was exported profitably to France. One-quarter of the Pontine marshes were drained for cultivation—a job that was finally finished by Mussolini in the 1920s. The Vatican Museum and library emerged better organized and expanded.

The French gave almost fanatic attention to the preservation of Roman ruins. The work was supervised by Canova and the director general of imperial museums, Baron Dominique Denon. Uncovering and restoring the Colosseum was a continuing project. The Arch of Titus was restored. The columns of the Temple of Vespasian were uncovered, as was the Column of Trajan, which required excavating debris 15 feet deep. Buildings, except churches, in the vicinity of the ruins were demolished to clear the view. Tons of earth and debris were removed to expose the Basilica of Constantine. A garden to beautify the surroundings of all the ruins was planned. It called for 76,000 trees for the Forum, Palatine Hill, and groves near the Colosseum and other ruins. Although it was not completed, it inspired work by later governments.

The Napoleonic government left physical reminders that are evident even today. Rome saw unprecedented efficiency and attempts at modernization. But at the time the efforts of the French were appreciated only by a minority.[15] Italian historians, however, now pay them tribute.

SPAIN   Joseph entered Spain sworn to uphold the Constitution of Bayonne (1808) approved by a Spanish National Junta called by Napoleon. (See pp. 72–73.) It provided for a single-chamber Cortes (parliament), including nobles and clergy appointed by the king. A majority, however, was to be elected indirectly by universal male suffrage, though there were property qualifications for the delegates. For Spain, even to have a constitution was radical. So was the single Cortes, much less one dominated by commoners. Provincial cortes, controlled by the privileged orders, were traditional.

The king was to have an appointive ministry, a council of state, and a senate. There was to be an independent judiciary. The tangle of royal, provincial, noble, and church courts were to be replaced by a unified system. Certain rights were guaranteed: equality of taxation and opportunity, equality before the law, jury trial (if the Cortes approved), and freedom from arbitrary arrest. Torture was forbidden, except under warrant. All feudal rights were abolished. Entail was made illegal for large estates. Internal tariffs were to be eliminated and guilds disbanded. To conciliate the powerful clergy, the Catholic church was declared established. After noting its part in the

---

[15] The best-received innovations were champagne and the waltz.

rebellion of 1808, however, Napoleon abolished the monastic orders and the Inquisition.

Joseph tried to govern in the spirit of the constitution, though war prevented implementing it. His continual references to it much irritated Napoleon. "Tell me," wrote the emperor in 1809, "if the Constitution prohibits the King of Spain from commanding 300,000 Frenchmen . . . if the Constitution says that at Saragossa [under seige] we may jump over the houses. . . ."

When conditions permitted, however, the king enforced the bill of rights. He organized his ministry, council of state, and senate as the constitution specified. Throughout, the ministry was all Spanish, even to the minister of war, Gonzalo O' Farrill. The most effective members were François (Francisco) de Cabarrús[16] (Finance) and Don Manuel Romero (Interior and Justice). Both had served the liberal Charles III (1759–1788), but had lost favor under Charles IV and been persecuted by the Inquisition. Joseph's few French advisers (e.g., Miot) were in the council of state, also overwhelmingly Spanish; the senate was totally so. Together they represented a pool of liberal talent rivaled only by the rebel Cortes at Cadiz, which sought vainly to direct the "patriot" cause. (See Chapter 6.)

Advised by Romero, Joseph planned a new administrative system—38 prefectures—with appointed prefects but elected councils with real power. New courts were planned as well. Neither the administration nor court system was installed, except temporarily in the Madrid area. The plans, however, became models for later governments.

Beyond the requirements of the constitution, Joseph attempted to foster a totally free economy. In his time laissez-faire principles were liberal—progressive. Not only did he abolish feudal privileges, guilds, and internal tariffs. The royal industries were put up for sale, including the crystal works at San Ildefonso, china works in Madrid, and tobacco and textile plants at various places. He abolished the royal monopolies—on manufacture and sale of tobacco, playing cards, liquor, wines, sealing wax, and on gambling.

[16] Born a Frenchman, but a Spanish count, he had founded the state Bank of Saint Charles. He was the father of the notorious Madame Tallien.

Since Bourbon overregulation had discouraged investment and innovation, this was expected to be beneficial. But in the midst of civil war, it only further disrupted the economy. Prices of monopoly items rose. Few buyers appeared for the industries. Some were closed; those sold were on credit. Unemployment increased, and with it sympathy for the rebels. Moreover, government revenues dropped. To bolster them Joseph reluctantly restored the royal monopolies and reintroduced internal tariffs.

Joseph had hoped to solve his budgeting problem and finance progressive projects by the liquidation of the confiscated national properties—mostly church property—valued at 10 billion reals.[17] The notes issued exclusively for their purchase circulated as money, however, and rapidly depreciated. By the end of Joseph's reign they were worthless. The national (Bourbon) debt was paid in paper, and some current expenses were met. But the king's deficits increased yearly. Napoleon, by 1813, had sent almost 4 billion reals in coin to Spain. Joseph was also thwarted in his hope that sales would increase peasant landownership. Speculators benefited most.

The king planned a tax system geared closely to ability to pay. Conditions, however, prevented its implementation. The government lived on a hand-to-mouth basis—on meager traditional revenues, loans from France, and the armies' confiscations.

Despite his financial distress, Joseph dreamed and fought for progress. He established national juntas for the supervision of public welfare programs—health, hospitals, orphans' homes, and homes for the aged. Mass vaccination for smallpox was decreed. programs were prepared for combating epidemics—plagues, generally cholera—to which Spain was especially susceptible. Institutions of charity were multiplied, absorbing much of the king's liquid capital.

Joseph also found funds to equip his capital with a new water system. His decorative fountains, set in public squares, are his most obvious monuments in Madrid. The Spanish guide

[17] Real = 0.27 francs; franc = 3.75 reals = $0.20. Figures are in vellon reals (15.06 to the peso). The colonial silver peso (piece of eight) of 8 reals was the exact equivalent in weight and value to the U.S. dollar.

books generally denegrate Joseph—he still is "Joe Bottle"—but nevertheless call him "King of the Plazas" and "King of the Fountains."

Joseph placed the universities and schools under a central junta. He planned a complete public school system, but established only individual schools in Madrid. Also in the capital a museum for machines and devices with laboratories and a school of geometry was founded. He had laid out the Royal Botanical Gardens, which still exist. Of lesser importance, he organized a Royal Opera Company, patronized the theaters, made courtiers of the leading playwrights of the day, and retained Goya as court painter.[18]

More startling, it was Joseph who converted the Prado palace into a museum of art. Now one of the world's greatest, its collection was begun with paintings and objects from the Royal Palace and works from confiscated monasteries. Joseph also began the restoration of the Alhambra of Granada, now one of the top tourist attractions in Spain.

The king opened careers to talent. His efforts benefited largely the middle class and lower nobility, however. Joseph's educational program was his main hope for social progress, and it required peace and more time than fate allowed him.

In Napoleon's eyes, Joseph spent too much time on his progressive plans; not enough on war. Joseph kept trying desperately to be more than king by conquest; "I can also be king by love of the Spanish," he wrote Napoleon. The emperor was much irritated; he appreciated Joseph's good intentions, but his projects could await peace. With guerrillas burning hospitals and torturing French prisoners—one general was boiled alive—he resented Joseph's wooing the Spanish and complaining of French atrocities. The king could not raise a Spanish army, pay French troops, or even balance his civil budget.

In 1810 the emperor limited Joseph's authority to New Castile, Avila, and Segovia. Joseph was appalled; Spain seemed almost conquered, and there were signs he was winning some popularity. Most of Spain was placed under military governors.

[18] The old man secretly painted his *Disasters of War,* which saved him from the wrath of Ferdinand VII in 1814.

Some were good, notably Louis Suchet in Aragon-Valenica. He crushed Spanish armies, destroyed guerrilla bands, governed wisely, and collected sufficient taxes to support himself and contribute to Joseph's treasury. But most of the governors were arbitrary, cruel, and despotic. In Joseph's opinion they embittered the Spanish, drove them into the arms of the guerrillas, and made total pacification daily more improbable. Surely he was right in part. The temper of the population was improving in 1810. When he was restored to command in 1812, it was more violent than ever. Of course in 1810 the French had been winning; Wellington held only Lisbon; the Spanish Cadiz and a few other strong points. Still public outrage toward the French helped Wellington to easy victory in 1813.

In peaceful circumstances, Joseph surely would have been a progressive and well-loved monarch. "He would have captivated the Spanish," wrote the former rebel Count José de Toreño, if Napoleon had not been in the background. With conditions as they were, he might have accomplished more—militarily and otherwise—without Napoleon's interference.

One thing seems certain: if Napoleon's government in Spain had operated as planned, it would not simply have robbed the country and drained off its manpower. It was formed to enlighten, educate, introduce organization and efficiency, and alter society.

THE ILLYRIAN PROVINCES   Created after Wagram (1809), made part of France, the Illyrian Provinces comprised the former Balkan lands of Austria taken in 1805 and 1809. (See p. 77.) The governor was Marshal Marmont, who had administered (1805–1809) Venetian "Dalmatia"—nominally for Eugène, in Italy—and added to it the Republic of Ragusa (1808), after saving it from the Russians.[19] He had devoted his time largely to the military and to road building—the latter with unusual success.

Administration had been in the hands of Vincenzo Dandolo, a rich Venetian Francophile who knew the area. From his capital at Zara, he gave Dalmatia a departmental organization

[19] Most accounts say Ragusa volunteered to become French. This is not quite accurate.

and a police force utilizing "pandours" (local militia) furnished by the villages—a practical system among wild mountaineers. At his order, the Code Napoléon, in Latin,[20] was proclaimed the law, but he did not enforce it, nor did he tamper with the feudal rights of the nobles. He did, however, bring the church under secular control, deprive it of its tithe, confiscate monastic property, and abolish most orders. He laid plans for a public school system. His greatest reform was the transfer of lands in the interior, nominally state property, to the peasants, whose feudal dues were converted into a tax. With the creation of the Illyrian Provinces, Dandolo withdrew from the government.

Marshal Auguste Marmont made Laibach his capital. The whole territory was organized into four departments but ruled in essentially racial divisions—a practical measure—by six intendants through subdelegates and *Anziani,* chiefs of rural districts, all appointed by the governor. Marmont was succeeded in 1811 by General Henri Bertrand; Andoche Junot, rapidly going insane, took over briefly in 1813; Fouché saw the Provinces through their final days.

Marmont and Bertrand extended Dandolo's reforms to the new territory, and went further. Feudalism was abolished in 1811. Nobles were to be reimbursed for only one-fifth of their financial losses out of new land taxes. The peasants, however, given a taste of freedom, refused to pay and armed themselves. Many nobles fled to Austria. Bertrand was forced to use troops to restore order. Feudalism disappeared, but the people gave the French no gratitude.

The governor forged ahead, nevertheless, proclaiming the Code Napoléon in full force in 1812, and restructuring the courts. The Code was never fully enforced, but its influence is evident in the Yugoslav law of the present day. A French-style tax system was more effectively enforced and the consolidated debt of the provinces partially liquidated by the use of confiscated church lands.

Public works were continued. Imperial highways were completed from Laibach to Fiume and Trieste and Karlovac to Ragusa, and Illyrians cooperated with Italian road builders

[20] Latin was the only language common to the nobles, lawyers, and clergy.

to link Trieste and Venice. Marmont and Bertrand were also able to produce a small army. Conscription never worked, but traditional local levies, most effective in Croatia, filled the ranks.

The Illyrian Provinces, however, were not a great asset to France. Nor were the French well-loved. The peasants were not grateful for the benefits conferred on them. The nobles resented the loss of their privileges. The middle-class merchants hated the Continental System. Smuggling was easy along the convoluted Adriatic coastline. Trieste and other large ports suffered, however, though in 1810 licenses were granted the Illyrians (technically French) before the Italians were supplied.

Napoleon recognized his failure in the Slavic lands. In 1812 he promised Illyria to Austria, upon Russia's defeat, in return for the remainder of Galicia (for Poland). He again bartered with Illyria in an attempt to maintain Austrian neutrality in 1813. Nevertheless, the Napoleonic legacy to the Balkans was considerable. Feudalism could never be totally restored; memory of the Code Napoléon and French administrative efficiency remained. The recognition of Serb and Croatian as official languages by Marmont served to promote general Slavic national pride. The struggles of the lower classes during the period raised hopes for greater national freedom in the future.

WESTPHALIA Jerome Bonaparte entered Westphalia with a new wife—Catherine of Württemberg.[21] Religious, well-educated, fluent in French, sturdy—the emperor wanted nephews —comely if not pretty, she seemed just right. She in fact proved a model queen, though she could never reform Jerome. To the king, twenty-three, handsome to the point of effeminacy, *cherchez la femme* was a way of life. But he proved an effective executive and military commander.

To insure the success of the kingdom, the emperor sent ahead of Jerome a team of French experts—Joseph Siméon, Jacques Beugnot, and Jean Jollivet—to organize it for him.

---

[21] He had married Elizabeth Patterson of Baltimore in 1803 and had an American son. Although the pope refused to annul the marriage, it was done by the Archbishop of Paris.

Jerome Bonaparte, king of Westphalia, 1807–1813. Napoleon's youngest brother and Europe's best-known playboy, he was an effective administrator and capable military commander. *(The New York Public Library)*

General Lagrange, who had been military governor in Hesse-Cassel since 1806, was made war minister. Surprisingly, however, it was the young king himself who made Westphalia an exemplary state.

A constitution was devised for Westphalia by Napoleon and Jean Jacques Cambacérès, advised by a hand-picked committee of Germans. The king was to rule with an appointed ministry and a council of state of 25. The ministers, from the start, were all German, with two exceptions—Siméon, minister of justice, who came to be accepted almost as a native, and, at Napoleon's insistence, the minister of war, a position held by various French generals.

The parliament (Ständeversammlung) was a single-chamber body of 100. It was elected by universal manhood suffrage through electors. A few peasants were even elected—admittedly, some as a joke. Incredibly, this body actually made law during the first three years of Jerome's reign. Then it became recalcitrant (1810) over war taxes, was dismissed and never called again.

The law was the Code Napoléon. Siméon, assisted by German law professors and judges, had a translation well under way before the king arrived. It went into effect on January 1, 1808. In the constitution and in the Code, feudalism, guilds, and entail were abolished, and there was the usual roster of rights.

For administration, there were eight departments, subdivided according to the French system. The prefects were Germans—one and all. Five were aristocrats; three from the middle class. The ratio in the ministry and council of state was also in favor of the nobles. This seemed practical for Westphalia, where the nobility was still highly respected. Napoleon let them take leadership while working for long-term social reform. Prefects, subprefects, mayors, and their councils were appointed by the king from rosters drawn up by departmental electoral colleges, which also nominated justices of the peace. The courts were organized on the French model.

Jerome was a good executive. He tried to pick capable men and let them do their jobs. Those who failed were replaced. He had a mind for essentials and did not allow himself to get bogged down in detail. His officials recognized his ability; so did his subjects. He was a little lazy—as most good executives are. He delegated authority freely, but never for a minute gave it up. When he worked he worked hard and thoroughly. When he was with the army, he took over. He knew his officers and his troops, and cared about them; they knew it.

As in Italy, the army, administration, and judiciary became instruments of social change. Commissions—and admission to military schools—were granted on merit. The officer corps remained mostly aristocratic, but the way was open for all. Prussians, Hessians, Hanovarians, Saxons, and others mingled in the military schools and in the ranks of the army. There was a "leveling" of the language. Men of all religions, similarly, marched together—Calvinists, Catholics, Lutherans, and Jews. Social mobility was promoted, and provincialism diminished. In the judiciary and the administration there was a similar effort to keep careers open to talent. The middle class made more progress there than in the military.

The story of finances in Westphalia is a sad one. The kingdom began with a debt that grew larger every year. The minister of finance, Hans von Bülow, managed to provide funds, however, without oppressive taxes, by selling the confiscated property of the churches, Catholic and Protestant, and by borrowing. Thus, although there was little building and few welfare projects, the kingdom served the Empire well, essential institutions were maintained, and there was considerable reform.

The churches lost all feudal rights, and their monastic property. All were subjected to governmental regulation. The Jews got unqualified rights of citizenship. They held public office and served as officers in the army—a first for Germany.

All schools were put under a director of education, the first, Johannes von Müller, an internationally known historian. In Prussian service in 1806, he had met Napoleon at Berlin, and had become a disciple. Westphalia had five universities and 3100 public schools already operating. Germany led, in this era, in public education. All the lower schools were kept open throughout the reign.

Müller, to his chagrin, had to close two universities

(Helmstedt and Rintln) to have funds for the others—Halle, Göttingen, and Marburg. Displaced professors who could not find positions were pensioned. Still, he had hoped when he died (1809) that Göttingen, his alma mater, would become a center of "new European culture" in Germany. New departments were added (e.g., French literature), but the faculty thought that Germans already excelled the French, particularly in science and philosophy—they were not altogether wrong—and resisted sweeping change.[22] Nevertheless, Jerome patronized the universities, though his infrequent anti-intellectual outbursts are often quoted.

At Göttingen, the king built an observatory for Karl Friedrich Gauss, after whom the unit of magnetic flux density is named. He appointed the distinguished Protestant theologian August Niemeyer rector at Marburg. There was a royal society (Societät für Wissenschaft) for professors and other intellectuals, French and German. Many prizes were offered. Jerome's government sponsored the publication of the first comprehensive German dictionary, that of Heinrich von Campe. His court librarian was Jakob Grimm, a philologist, but later famous for the *Fairy Tales* (with brother Wilhelm).

There was some trouble in the universities, including student riots, but seldom over political matters. The first occurred when Jerome suppressed the dueling societies. But the students soon learned it was more fun to plant scars-of-honor in secret. (No German government has ever been able to eliminate dueling, including the present one in West Germany.) In 1809 a few were motivated very briefly by pan-German nationalism, but this became important only after 1815. Students generally welcomed Jerome and, as might be expected, stood in awe of his bad reputation. "A Roman circus," old Goethe had said after one of his parties! They also appreciated that he had a German government. Professors made snide remarks in private, but those few who really opposed him left the country. The new University of Berlin (1810) needed a whole faculty.

[22] Göttingen became famous for physics in the nineteenth century. In the 1920s and 1930s it trained many men who were later key figures in the U.S. atomic program, including Robert Oppenheimer (an American), Edward Teller (Austrian), and Enrico Fermi (Italian). The university has revived since World War II.

Jerome's public welfare programs never really got beyond the planning stage. The public debt was too heavy; the demands of Napoleon constantly increasing. However, existing hospitals and charitable institutions were kept going. The minister of the interior supervised the health program, including the enforcement of smallpox vaccination.

In terms of contribution to the Empire, Westphalia ranked with Italy. The kingdom was stable. Jerome supported an army of 25,000, and French troops as well. He mustered 38,000 in 1812, of which 22,000 served in Russia; few returned. In addition he sent 13,000 men to Spain, and raised 20,000 to fight for Napoleon in 1813. The kingdom was overrun in 1813, but Jerome's Guard escorted him to the Rhine, and some of his men fought on with Napoleon. Everywhere Westphalians distinguished themselves. Ninety-three won the Legion of Honor in Russia.

The efficiency of his government, his reforms, and the French institutions he introduced left a lasting impression. In the nineteenth century, the first revolutions in Germany were in areas once part of Westphalia.

HOLLAND   Louis Bonaparte was a man of great compassion, who in his short reign won the hearts of his subjects. Afflicted with many ills—probably mostly psychosomatic—he was flabby, balding, and looked older than Napoleon, who was nine years his senior. Married against his will to the lovely blonde Hortense de Beauharnais, he lived apart from her, even when residing in the same palace. They had three sons, however, before they separated (1810). The last, Louis Napoleon, became Napoleon III. A half-time king, he nonetheless displayed, when well, energy, intelligence, imagination, and a quiet courage—the sort which took him into plague areas to help the victims.

The constitution of Holland provided for a legislature of 38 men, the existing "High Mightinesses" plus royal appointees. There was a roster of civil liberties. Freedom of religion, traditional in Holland, was affirmed. Dutch was to remain the official language. The independence and territorial integrity of Holland were guaranteed.

The constitution also promised Holland favored economic treatment by France, which was confirmed by treaties.

Louis Bonaparte, king of Holland, 1806–1810. He became a Dutch nationalist, and was driven from his throne by Napoleon. Despite ill health and his short tenure, he made many reforms in his kingdom, and is well remembered by Dutch historians. *(The New York Public Library)*

But Napoleon's policies varied with the degree of Louis's enforcement of the Continental System. Once he forbade trade with Holland in colonial goods altogether—even those from Dutch colonies—until regulations were tightened.

To Louis, the Continental System was "immoral." He issued appropriate orders, but seldom checked to see if Dutch officials complied with them. This, however, was not the only thing that irritated Napoleon. Louis consulted his legislature about everything. Even when he issued emergency decrees during epidemics and floods, he submitted them for confirmation. To the emperor's objection, Louis replied, "Does Your Majesty not rule with his senate?"

On the abolition of feudalism, Louis also dragged his feet. The guilds were spared, though placed under regulation. The king used only parts of the Code Napoléon, which, said he, was un-Dutch. Moreover, Louis ruled against conscription because the Dutch had never had compulsory military service. Few Dutch would volunteer, so he employed mercenaries, mostly German. To give the army a national character he decreed that orders be given in Dutch, but it remained a foreign legion, though of the size, roughly, Napoleon required. Until 1810 the emperor tolerated Louis's policy. Holland still "lent" him money and the Dutch navy, an object of national pride, was excellent.

The Dutch government lived on loans. Its borrowings averaged 104 million florins a year; its tax income, 53 million.[23] In 1809 the interest on the debt was 48 million. Because in effect the people with the money were in the government, the king's credit remained good. They preferred supporting him, collecting interest, and perhaps eventually their capital, to reforming taxes.

Louis spent millions on dikes and reclaiming cultivable land from the sea and marshes. He also had a grand scheme for eliminating the winter floods which broke dams, inundated towns, destroyed property, took lives, and left disease in their wake. On the advice of radical Dutch hydraulic engineers, Louis suggested that dikes on the Meuse (Maas) and Waal be systematically sluiced every year at flood time, allowing the water to

[23] Florin = 2.17 francs.

flow overland to the sea. Structures were to be put on piles in predicted flood lanes and people and stock moved as necessary. Disasters would be avoided, and alluvium left to enrich the soil. This was too extreme for the Dutch at the time, but by 1825 they had adopted the system, and still use it, in part.

Louis centralized control of public instruction, including the six universities, though their independence was scarcely impaired. He founded a royal society. The existing public schools were kept in operation.

The Dutch had virtually "invented" religious toleration. But in some localities Protestants—generally in the majority— discriminated against Catholics, usually with respect to taxation and use of public facilities. And in a few places where Catholics predominated the reverse was true. Louis undertook to "fight both ways." "When I am in Catholic territory, I am a Protestant," he said, "and when in Protestant areas, I am a Catholic." He personally investigated complaints and ordered injustices remedied on the spot.

The king's greatest personal crusade, however, was for the improvement of public health, perhaps motivated partly by his own suffering. He organized a national council for public health, planned for epidemic control, enforced smallpox vaccination, and went much further. His most grandiose scheme, which was never implemented, was for an international center for the collection of medical knowledge which would then be distributed worldwide. In this Louis was a century before his time.

Some of his programs drew laughs—for example, a campaign for breast-feeding babies. But he was dead serious and concerned about his people. He went into epidemic areas and sat by bedsides through the night. To the consternation of professionals, he also often took control of rescue and relief in flood areas. The people admired him for it.

Napoleon, however, was not pleased with Louis; the king was too Dutch. Using nonenforcement of the Continental System as an excuse, he drove him from his throne in 1810, as already noted. There was little sentiment for inviting Louis back after Napoleon's fall, but Dutch historians have treated him kindly.

GRAND DUCHY OF BERG   The Duchy, later Grand Duchy, of Berg was created for Murat after Austerlitz (1805) from the duchies of Cleves and Berg, respectively Prussian and Bavarian, exchanged for other territory. With the creation of the Confederation of the Rhine (1806), and again after Tilsit (1807) it was further enlarged.[24] The capital was Düsseldorf, and it included the Ruhr, already a center of mining and metalworking.

The state was a reward to Murat for his military services. For Caroline Bonaparte, his wife, it was all too little. Unwilling to be buried in "rustic" Düsseldorf, she pursued Napoleon, constantly bidding for a kingdom until she got Naples (1808) for herself and Murat. (See p. 73.) Murat, perpetually on military assignment, had spent little time in Berg. In 1809 Napoleon Louis Bonaparte, son of Louis, age five, was named Grand Duke. The state was really governed by Napoleon's administrators from the beginning. Much property, including forests and mines, was, in any case, part of the imperial domains.

The duchy was organized in 1806 by Agar, who later served Murat in Naples. Local diets were eliminated; the state was divided into districts under appointed councillors, most of whom were German nobles. Mayors of cities were picked from lists presented by existing city councils. A common land tax was added to those of the former states, and conscription was introduced; there had been no draft in the Prussian lands.

In 1809 Jacques Claude Beugnot, transferred from Westphalia, reformed the tax system, abolished guilds, and legalized marriage between nobles and commoners. He remained a minister of finances when (1810) Pierre Louis Roederer (formerly in Naples) became chief administrator. Roederer restructured the courts and in 1812 issued a constitution, formed a council of state, and named an assembly of notables.

Meanwhile, the churches were taken under civil control and the clergy put on salary. The usual demise of the monastic orders followed. Roederer planned a university for Düsseldorf,

[24] Additions were Nassau, Dillenberg, Mark, the city of Lippenstadt, Prussian Münster, Tecklenberg, and Lingen. Murat also got the postal monopoly of north Germany, held since 1615 by the house of Thurn and Taxis.

but went no further. He did establish three *lycées,* but otherwise just kept the existing lower schools operating.

Serfdom and feudalism were abolished in 1808, but dues were made redeemable. The Code Napoléon was introduced, belatedly, in 1811. The peasants thereupon refused to pay feudal dues, which were clearly unlawful. Napoleon, however, unwilling to alienate the aristocracy in view of the Russian crisis, ruled against them. Peasant delegations to Paris were arrested on their return. The nobles' right to compensation for "money rights," with minor exceptions, was reaffirmed.

The peasants benefited greatly, nevertheless, from the decrees of 1809–1811. Property distribution was accelerated as perhaps nowhere else in the Empire. The advice of French agricultural experts was heeded, which resulted in crop improvement. New roads were built, providing better access to market. Most important, feudalism was gone forever; the Prussian government did not restore it after 1815.

At first, the economy of Berg declined. It's most famous product, Remscheid steel, lost its markets. It had been exported worldwide to shipyards, barrel factories, needleworks, tool plants, and the like. Next in importance were textiles, which depended on the importation of wool from Spain and England, silk from Italy, and cotton from the United States, the Spanish colonies, the Levant, and elsewhere.

The steel industry was able to convert to manufacturing for imperial needs—especially of war—and though it suffered in the early years, was greatly expanded by 1812. Textiles, impeded by French tariffs, declined steadily, and workers who could find other work emigrated in droves. Overall, however, the economy was reoriented permanently, and for the "new Germany," beneficially. The Ruhr "took off" as an iron-steel-machinery, and less happily, arms-producing center. Its industry has continued to thrive to this day, despite the destruction of two world wars.

Napoleonic rule brought economic adjustments in Berg which hurt many individuals. Taxes were high. Conscription was not joyfully received, and was rejected, amid rioting, after half the duchy's 5000-man army was lost in Russia.

In the balance, however, the gains for Berg outweighed the losses. Industry grew, feudalism disappeared, and peasant landholding increased. Moreover, the Prussian king, after 1815, retained the French-style administration and courts and left the Code Napoléon virtually in full force.

GRAND DUCHY OF FRANKFURT With the creation of the Rhein-bund (1806), the one church state left from the Holy Roman Empire, Frankfurt, was given to the Prince Primate of Germany, Charles Theodore Dalberg, later Grand Duke. After his death, it was to go to Eugène de Beauharnais. (See p. 79.) The imposing former Archbishop-Elector of Mainz, a sincere "man of 1789," had welcomed the French invasion of the Rhineland. Lefebvre calls him a "good Catholic and a good German," but a Josephist (follower of Joseph II, d. 1790, the enlightened Austrian emperor).

Dalberg's chief ministers were Baron Albini and Count Beust, both German. He promulgated a constitution and formed a council of state and an "Estates" (legislature) named by electors he himself appointed. The Grand Duchy included the city of Frankfurt (on the Main) and environs, Aschaffenburg, Fulda, and Hanau. A French-style administration was installed. Equality of taxation and freedom of religion were proclaimed; feudalism was declared abolished and guilds disbanded.

The Code Napoléon, however, was not the law until 1810, and was enforced by traditional courts that were not totally reformed until 1813. All the while, local seigneural courts and church courts continued to function. The churches came under state control and the monastic orders disappeared. But religious freedom was limited by Dalberg's requirement of church marriage, Catholic or Protestant, which violated the civil code. Jews were not given full citizenship until 1812. Until then, though authorized to own land and operate industries, they had to live in specified locations—ghettos. Until 1811 they had to pay special taxes (1813 for Fulda and Aschaffenburg). Jews were nevertheless appointed to high office and exerted influence. Amschel Rothschild, the *pater familias* of the international banking clan, was made an elector.

Nobles retained their titles and in rural areas their juridical rights. The picture on feudal dues, however, was mixed. Although nominally abolished without compensation in Fulda and Hanau (1808), the peasants were everywhere forced to buy their freedom by village, and many declined. Compensation had to be paid even on ducal or confiscated lands. The Code Napoléon made feudalism illegal, but it persisted, in part. Serfdom, ended by imperial decree, did not entirely disappear.

Frankfurt was far from being a model progressive state, but for Germany, its record was good. The government was efficient, the administration honest, and the people reasonably satisfied. Napoleonic ideals were upheld as a goal, if not forcefully applied. Feudalism was on the way to extinction. Society was to some degree modernized. The number of peasant proprietors increased.

GRAND DUCHY OF WARSAW   "I want a camp in Poland, not a forum," Napoleon once said in anger. He spoke the truth. What he got, however, was both. Polish troops were among his most reliable; the Polish lancers of the Imperial Guard made legend; Poniatowski became one of the 26 marshals of France. But the chambers of the duchy's government excelled in the production of words, not deeds.

Created from Prussian Poland after Tilsit (1807), the Grand Duchy was placed under King Frederick Augustus of Saxony. Said he, "I do my best; for the rest I trust in God and the Emperor." Old, painfully religious, sedentary and indecisive, he seldom left Dresden. His court, said the vivacious Polish Countess Potocki "resembled that of sleeping beauty."

The French Baron Bignon, Napoleon's "resident," repeatedly proposed that he re-create the Polish kingdom under a Bonaparte. But the emperor temporized. He knew that all the nobility wanted a kingdom, but violently disagreed over the form. As it was, he had the support of Prince Adam Czartoryski, head of The Family, most of its members—though young Adam served the tsar—and most other great nobles. They accepted French domination as best under the circumstances, at least until 1813. Moreover, Napoleon did not care to alienate the tsar, while allied with him, by strengthening Poland. After 1810 he hoped the tsar would come to terms more easily if he left the Polish question open.

The Grand Duchy was ruled by a ministry of great nobles at Warsaw, one of whom maintained liaison with the Saxon king at Dresden. The state's constitution, modeled after the French, was published by Napoleon himself in 1807. Beneath the ministry was an appointive council of state and a senate of 18—6 bishops, 12 laymen—and an elected diet of 160. All were named by nobles. The diet was supposed to have a popular contingent from the cities and towns, but only "citizens" qualified for election, and the word had been translated "landholder." The diet met three times, briefly. The other chambers were dominated by arch-conservatives. Despite these facts, the ministry, along with "play-acting" for Napoleon, made some real advances.

Very early Count Stanislas Potocki emerged as president of the council of ministers. Elderly, tall, very thin, elegant, traveled, multilingual, he was a figurehead agreeable to all parties. An aristocrat, enormously rich, married to a Czartoryski, he was at the same time Grand Master of Freemasons in Poland, whose arms bore the Napoleonic "N".[25] By instinct, he protected noble privileges, while declaiming, with utmost sincerity, on the glories of progress. This suited his ministers, who in council were called the "seven sleeping brothers," and outside did as they liked.

The most important man in the Duchy to Napoleon was Prince Joseph Poniatowski, minister of war, who sent him troops and commanded a strong Polish army. "There was a Pole [out of legend]," says the French historian Abel Mansuy, "without qualification . . . an accomplished cavalier, a prince charming."

---

[25] Freemasonry had vague origins in medieval stonemason's guilds, which supported charities. The modern lodges originated in Britain and spread to the Continent. National lodges of the eighteenth century promoted the ideals of the Enlightenment. That of France, of which the Duke d'Orléans was Grand Master and Lafayette a member, was suspected of fomenting the Revolution, but was destroyed by it. Napoleon revived the order in France. European Freemasons generally supported him.

He had fought in 1794 with Thaddeus Kosciusko—of American Revolutionary fame—for a free Poland, but resigned himself to the partition of Poland among Russia, Austria, and Prussia. In 1806, however, Napoleon's victory over the Prussians convinced him that backed by France Poland might live again. He gave his allegiance to Napoleon, and died fighting for him in 1813. Politically, he was not a power. But few men in Poland were more highly respected—or more loved by the ladies.

The most ardent reformer was the minister of interior, Count John Paul Luszczewski. No grand seigneur but a protégé of the French, small and fat, his life was hard and he died in office. He succeeded, nevertheless, in installing a departmental administration and populating it in part with nonnobles. The prefectures he organized lasted until 1830.

Serfdom was abolished, but the former serfs received no land. They had the choice of leaving the land or remaining as rent-paying tenants, subject directly to taxes and feudal dues, which were not abolished. Those who left became day laborers, joined the proletariat of the cities—none very large, and lacking industry—where employment was hard to find, or became vagabonds or bandits. In some areas the nobles took advantage of the law to expel unneeded laborers (or troublemakers). Nevertheless, the peasantry was freed, and opportunities for the enterprising increased.

An embryonic middle class appeared between that of the nobles and of the peasants. It comprised the stewards of the nobles—some of whom did the actual work of prefects, subprefects, and mayors—military officers who rose from the ranks in the French or Polish armies, merchants, artisans and some nonnoble proprietors.

There was no radical change in society. But the Continental System accelerated the impoverishment of the old aristocracy, whose fortunes depended on agriculture, by closing, especially, overseas grain markets. They sold off land, ultimately profitable again, to rising new men. Moreover, the system promoted industry—notably in textiles, metals, and distilling—and mining, which gave money and status to nonnoble enterprisers. Still, nobles retained control of the country, and though liberty and equality were proclaimed, Napoleonic principles were not applied.

Unlike Luszczewski, most ministers were "patriots," who meant to serve Poland, trimming their sails as the balance of power demanded. Typical was the minister of police, Count Ignatius Sobolewski, a debonnaire seigneur who kept on good terms with both Poniatowski and young Adam Czartoryski (in Russia).

Of like mind was the minister of justice and cults, Count Felix Lubienski, who made a great show of installing the Code Napoléon, reforming the courts, and bringing the church under secular control. But the promulgation of the Code was celebrated by a *Te Deum* in Warsaw, clearly forecasting that the church would supervise its application. He reformed the courts, but the judges he appointed were in vast majority noble, rich, and unsympathetic toward the Code, which was translated into Polish, but not enforced. In 1812, Lubienski and the minister of finance, Thaddeus Matuszewisz, were among the first to defect to the victorious Russians.

The church, throughout, was a bulwark of reaction. Conscious of its power over the people, Napoleon compromised at the beginning. In the constitution he declared the "Christian, Apostolic and Roman" Church established, contradicting the declaration of religious freedom in the same document. Moreover, he did not replace the ultraconservative primate of Poland, Ignatius Raczyński, who had assumed office on becoming senior archbishop.

Raczyński resided at the château of Ciazno, closer to Dresden than Warsaw, and kept the pious king of Saxony subject by his towering presence and iron will. He rejected civil marriage and divorce out of hand. He retained the property of the church intact. Church courts continued to function as usual. He induced the king to suspend that part of the constitution which gave the Jews full citizenship and the right to public worship. They received civil rights only upon payment and grant of patent and required special permission to buy land.

The minister of "cults" quailed before the primate. The influence of the clergy in the council of state and senate at

Warsaw was disproportionate to their numbers. There were vocal liberal nobles—among them Dombrowski, who since 1795 had led a Polish legion in the French army. Liberal clergymen, however, were soon silenced by Raczyński.

In Saint Petersburg, the persuasive Adam Czartoryski worked for a Polish kingdom under the tsar. In 1811, after Alexander broke with Napoleon, and the other partitioning powers—Prussia and Austria—stood with France, the tsar gave in. He offered Warsaw a Polish-Lithuanian kingdom with an outlet to the sea, a liberal constitution, and maximum autonomy. The offer was refused; Napoleon's power seemed too great to oppose. But the Polish nobility was badly divided, not only between Francophiles and Russophiles, but between conservatives and liberals. A few still dreamed of true Polish independence.

In the spring of 1812, while Napoleon's armies assembled for the Russian campaign, he took steps to counter the tsar's offer. At his behest, the elder Prince Adam Czartoryski presided over an extraordinary *Zeym* at Warsaw which founded a new Polish Confederation. Simultaneously the emperor sent an ambassador—the rank appropriate to kingly courts—to Warsaw. And finally, Jerome Bonaparte arrived as commander of the right wing of the Grande Armée. Many, including Jerome, thought he would be named king of Poland.

Napoleon, however, took no further action. Jerome marched with the army. Apparently the emperor judged Polish opinion still too divided. And for the moment he had what he wanted from Poland—Poniatowski and 90,000 disciplined Polish troops.

In terms of progress and enlightenment, the Grand Duchy of Warsaw cannot be rated very highly. Nevertheless its government was superior to that it replaced, and its example undoubtedly influenced the tsar to grant a constitution to the Kingdom of Poland created in 1815.

The memory of the Code Napoléon, however poorly enforced, remained to inspire revolutionaries. Society had been shaken, inviting change. The industrial sector of the economy had gained strength. French administrative, judicial, and financial systems operated until the disastrous revolution of 1830 against Russia. Polish nationalism, reborn under Napoleon, increased in reaction to Russian tyranny after 1815, and more so after 1830. In their soul-despair the people memorialized the heroism of the Poles of the Grande Armée.

After World War I, when Poland finally became independent, a huge mural of the charge of the Poles at Somo Sierra (1808), in Spain, was installed in the House of the Diet. It celebrated not only Polish bravery, but victory in a century-long struggle for freedom in which the lancers of the Imperial Guard were seen as true patriots.

CONCLUSION   The common factors in the governance of the satellite states are obvious. All were established by force or threat of force and so held, in whole or part. Political opposition was silenced. But all had constitutions or came under the constitution of France. None was ever fully applied, but in every state there was some popular participation in government. In varying degree, the rights stated were enforced and reforms promised were effected. Governments, administrations, and judiciaries were remade, feudalism and serfdom were abolished. Equality before the law and of taxation, careers open to talent and freedom of religion became the rule. Everywhere, the Code Napoléon became the law, except in Spain, which was not unaffected by it. The churches lost property and their direct political power, except in Poland, and even there, under the law. Free domestic economies were fostered and landownership widened —even in Spain and Poland. There was a concentrated effort to promote the public welfare, to improve public health, and to promote education, science, the arts, and literature. Roads, bridges, canals, and harbors were built or improved. Cities got new water and sewage systems. Holland got new dikes; land was reclaimed there and elsewhere. There was also a determined attempt to sponsor social revolution. Because of the Empire's short life, this worked mostly to the advantage of the rising middle class. Public education, in time, however, would have allowed more men from the lower ranks of society to move up.

Napoleon, in short, sponsored revolution. This was one of the reasons for his downfall. The old rulers, the old privileged classes, naturally opposed the "crowned Jacobin." So, sooner or later, did those who stood to benefit most in the long run— the peasants and workers—impelled by traditional ideas and wounded by Napoleonic taxes, conscription, and the loss of their sons in war. Napoleon left them a legacy all the same.[26]

[26] Some of the most recent scholarship on Napoleonic states is found in: Centre d'Histoire Économique et Sociale, *Occupants-Occupés: 1792–1815* (Bruxelles: 1969), and *La France à l'époque Napoléonienne* (Numero Special), *Revue d'Histoire Moderne et Contemporaine,* XVII (Juillet 1970).

CHAPTER SIX

Challenge and Response

IMPACT WORLDWIDE Napoleon's influence was not confined to his satellite states. His conquest of Spain pushed the rebel government into Cadiz, where liberals took control and attempted reforms. In Prussia, the king approved far-reaching social and military reforms in an effort to strengthen the country. For the same reason, Austria briefly toyed with popular nationalism; in Germany and Italy, intellectuals began preaching national unification. The states of the Confederation of the Rhine adopted some French institutions. Napoleon's machinations weakened the Ottoman empire and promoted nationalism in the Balkans and Greece. Persia suffered from his interference; Egypt benefited from the French example. His policies affected events in Africa and the Far East.

The French emperor's abortive colonial

schemes resulted in the creation in Haiti of the first modern black-ruled state and delivered Louisiana to the United States. The American Republic, its commerce menaced on the one hand by Napoleon's Continental System and on the other by Britain's Orders in Council, nevertheless emerged richer and stronger than ever. The French invasion of Portugal sent the king into exile in Brazil, where his residence inspired a new sense of importance and paved the way for independence.

Meanwhile, the almost total conquest of Spain set its colonies adrift. They refused to recognize the kingship of Joseph Bonaparte, while paying scant attention to the weak rebel government. Some achieved independence; in others there were revolutions which presaged greater ones to come.

It is with these matters that this chapter will deal.

SPAIN In 1808 the objectives of Spanish liberals regarding reform were all but identical to those of Joseph Bonaparte. Notwithstanding, the majority plumped for the rebels. Perhaps most thought Joseph sincere, but distrusted Napoleon, and felt the king could accomplish little because of the anti-French fury of the masses. Some who pledged loyalty to Joseph at Bayonne (e.g., Pedro Cevallos and the duke d'Infantado) left him after his retreat from Madrid (July 1808).

The liberal rebels hoped to steer their government into a progressive course. They trumpeted to Britain and Europe the news of Bailén, the exploits of the guerrillas, and the resistance of Zaragoza—twice besieged; taken from starving people still fighting in the rubble, with their leader, José de Palafox, ill and unconscious. Men such as the Count de Toreño, Gaspar Jovellanos (d. 1811), Muñoz Torrero, Augustin Argüelles, and others, depicted the Spanish resistance as a liberal-nationalist struggle, which it was not.

The liberals' hour of triumph came in 1810 when the rebel regency was chased into Cadiz, there to remain under blockade until 1812. Under liberal guidance a Cortes was assembled to write a new constitution and assumed direction of the regency. Supposedly elected, most of the members were self-appointed, since the French controlled most of the Peninsula. It was a liberal body, because the progressives alone were organized and interested in reform. It was supported by the radical workers of the port—Francophobes and politically more sophisticated than the general peasant population.

The British welcomed the appearance of the Cortes, happy to deal with professed progressives rather than the stiff-backed reactionaries of the former governments. It did not escape them that the actual rebel leaders, in the field, paid scant attention to the Cortes's orders except when receipt of British supplies and arms were involved. It suited them to believe that they were supporting a New Spain—not the return of absolute monarchy, feudalism, and the Inquisition. In any case, the defeat of Napoleon had first priority.

The Cortes's Constitution of 1812 was an exercise in one-upmanship on Joseph's Bayonne document. It proclaimed the sovereignty of the people, civil, personal, and tax equality, and the inviolability of private property. It provided for a hereditary constitutional monarchy, a single-chamber Cortes elected by universal manhood suffrage, ministerial responsibility, and the separation of executive, legislative, and judicial powers.

The liberals had gambled that Ferdinand VII would accept the constitution when he returned. He did not. Wary on his reentry (March 1814), he gave the reformers hope, but within weeks reasserted his absolute powers—to the plaudits of the populace. Liberals fled or were jailed or executed. A few heads were exhibited in the cities to make the king's position clear.

Ferdinand, however, could not execute the Constitution of 1812. When revolution broke out in 1820, he was forced to accept it, if temporarily. Meanwhile it had become a model for other revolutionaries in Europe and Latin America. The progressive opponents of Napoleon, as well as the *afrancesados*, who sided with Joseph Bonaparte, contributed to the cause which the French emperor promoted.

PRUSSIA In 1807 Frederick William of Prussia gave almost dictatorial power to reform his truncated kingdom to the Baron Heinrich F. Karl vom und zum Stein, a native of Nassau, in the Rhineland. A former minister, now middle-aged, with a mane of greying hair and angry hooded eyes, he had earlier been too radical for the Junkers of the court—and still had enemies. Now Napoleon recommended him, however, as did the man he replaced, Count (later Prince) Karl August von Hardenberg. The emperor had taken the word of Pierre Daru, his civil administrator in the conquered lands, that Stein was enlightened, and, more important, capable of reordering Prussian finances and paying off the French indemnity. He did not realize Stein's intense hatred of the French, expressed long before his family's estates were lost in the reorganizations of Germany.

Stein was an odd combination of progressive and romantic. He was not a Prussian but a German nationalist; his ideal Germany, however, was the Holy Roman Empire of the twelfth century. His reforms were directed toward increasing popular loyalty and motivated not by sympathy for the masses, but for the state. He and Hardenberg, who advised him and returned to the ministry in 1810, agreed on the need for reform, but for different reasons. Hardenberg, a Hanovarian educated at Göttingen, an admirer of British institutions and disciple of Adam Smith, even looked the part of an English lord. Unlike Stein, he was a Prussian nationalist. Neither belong in the same category with Ernst Moritz Arndt, J. G. Fichte, Friedrich Ludwig Jahn, and other liberal proponents of a German nation-state.

Stein's program included four major reforms: (1) the abolition of serfdom, (2) the introduction of city councils elected by taxpayers to replace those of self-appointed merchant oligarchies, (3) the reorganization of the ministry, and (4) the creation of a national parliament (Landtag). He was successful in accomplishing the first two, though the final steps were taken by Hardenberg, who was again made chancellor in 1810.

Stein was ousted from his ministry (November 1808) on the demand of Napoleon, barely a year after his entering office. One of his many enemies at court had seen to it that a letter of Stein's, encouraging anti-French war propaganda, reached the emperor. Before he retired—to Vienna, then to St. Petersburg—however, Stein got the king's signature on his municipal and agrarian reform acts. The former went into effect without delay.

Serfs were freed, though not without qualification until

1810. The corvée and feudal dues remained. But landholding became the right of all classes, as did entry into any profession or occupation. By Hardenberg's further decree of 1811 all dues and obligations were canceled on cession to the nobles of part of the peasants' lands. Lords retained police power in small towns and some judicial rights over their former subjects. But a strong start had been made toward destroying feudalism. Hardenberg, moreover (1810–1811), carried through the abolition of compulsory membership in guilds, a boon to free enterprise, instituted freedom of contract, and emancipated the Jews.

The defeat of Napoleon ended further domestic reform, and there was some backsliding. But the trend started by Stein and Hardenberg could not be stayed indefinitely.

More important for the immediate future, Stein approved military reforms, proposed and carried out by Generals Gerhard Johann von Scharnhorst and August von Gneisenau, aided by younger officers including the later famous Karl von Clausewitz. The Krümpersystem was introduced, under which men were rotated into the army for training and released to a ready reserve. By this method the standing forces were kept at 42,000, as specified by Napoleon, but the army in 1812 numbered 150,000.

The appearance in 1813 of a Prussian army that could win victories was what really stirred the spirit of the people. Even then, there was no widespread mass movement against the French after the announcement by King Frederick William III that Prussia had joined the Allies (March 1813). The regular army did most of the fighting, aided by some draftees (1814), but conscription was temporary. The king feared a "nation at arms."

Prussia had, however, reformed itself in reaction to Napoleon's challenge. In the short run, therefore, Prussia's reforms were the most permanent in Germany, save those made in the Rhine provinces directly under French control.

AUSTRIA   Austria saw its only "national revival" in 1809, which for a polyglot empire of German, Slavs, Hungarians, and others, was remarkable. It was based purely on military reforms, the expansion of the regular and reserve forces, and whipping up antagonism for the French. It was short-lived. Napoleon, after he again conquered Vienna, went about almost unguarded.

The Emperor Francis, even more than the Prussian king, had feared the consequences of stirring up, in his case, various peoples. He cooperated only under the influence of his beautiful new wife and the Archduke Charles—himself won over by the romantic Heinrich von Kleist—who was convinced the Germans would rally to Austria's support. No such support appeared, of course. Francis was never a German nationalist. His interest in the "German War" was that it might make him Holy Roman Emperor again. That hope was exploded by Napoleon's victory at Wagram (July 1809).

Count Philipp Stadion, the chancellor, had entertained Stein-like plans for further reforms after the victory. Instead he found himself replaced by Clemens von Metternich. The emperor returned to a policy of reactionism. Metternich guided the state on a course of cooperation with Napoleon (including a marriage for him with an Austrian archduchess). In 1812 he signed an alliance committing troops to Napoleon for the Russian campaign. Always, however, he was waiting for the moment when Austria could break free of the French yoke. It came in 1813, and he took it happily, ranging Austria with the growing Allied coalition. In terms of reform, Austria, of all the states of Europe, was least affected by Napoleon's revolutionary example.

PAN-GERMANISM   The defeat of Austria in 1809 made the pan-Germans look to Prussia for leadership, though they got little official encouragement. The propagandists for German unity continued their work in Berlin. Ludwig von Arnim established his "German Christian Roundtable," from which "French, Jews, and philistines" were excluded. Heinrich von Kleist published his *Berliner Abendblätter*. Fichte and Ernst Moritz Arndt penned their propaganda, Friedrich Jahn founded his gymnastic societies, patriots worked in the universities to promote the *Tugendbund*, which collapsed around 1810 and revived only after 1815 in the form of the *Burschenschaften*.

The pan-German movement existed largely in the minds of intellectuals. Among the major leaders, Jahn alone could boast that he had produced fighters for the War of Liberation of 1813–1814. Wilhelm von Humboldt—naturalist, geographer, and founder of the University of Berlin—like Stein, would have preferred to see Germany return to its loose, federative political structure. A nation-state, he thought, would warp the outlook of German intellectuals, traditionally international, and endanger European peace.

Others treasured the old cultural atmosphere and had looked to Napoleon to safeguard it. Johann Schiller's son refused to fight the French in 1813. The giant of the romantics, Wolfgang von Goethe, forbade his son to fight in the War of Liberation—though he did, briefly—and wore the French Legion of Honor, even to receive an Austrian field marshal. G. W. F. Hegel vocally regretted Napoleon's fall—a Titan, he said, brought down by small-minded fools. We have noted the attitude of Johannes von Müller, Jakob Grimm, and others.

Nowhere, until after the Russian debacle, did cooperation with the French become disreputable. As history was to unfold, neither the romantic nor liberal intellectuals, but especially not the latter, would have much to do with the unification of Germany, which would be wrought by men of "blood and iron."

CONFEDERATION OF THE RHINE   In the states which were merely allied with France—not directly controlled, like Westphalia, Berg, and Frankfurt—Napoleon's ambassadors were not ragingly successful in bringing about reforms. He might have applied more pressure except for the crying need, always present, for German troops and supplies to maintain French garrisons. Nevertheless there were two states that made notable progress— Württemberg and Bavaria. Baden, which we shall not discuss, ran a close third.

The Elector Frederick of Württemberg (king after 1805) quarreled early with his parliament (Landtag). When it refused taxes to support Napoleon's 1805 campaign, Frederick took the emperor's from-the-saddle advice—"*Chassez-moi les bou-*

gres . . ."—and never called it again. He and his chief minister, Ferdinand von Wintzingerode, however, dictated a series of admirable reforms.

Administration and justice were centralized after the French fashion. Adaptations of the Napoleonic codes were instituted. Serfdom was abolished. The government and judicial functions of the nobles, together with their right to tax, were eliminated. Some feudal dues and the corvée remained. But landownership became the privilege of anyone, and noble-commoner marriages were legalized. The churches—the largest was the Lutheran—lost both feudal rights and monastic property, and were put under state supervision. Religious toleration was enforced. Jews, however, did not get full citizenship, though like all others, they could hold land and enter any profession. Schools, from the University of Tübingen down, were brought under royal control.

Though the state remained despotic in form, and the nobles continued to dominate society, Württemberg was much altered in its institutions and social patterns during the Napoleonic period.

In Bavaria, under the well-loved "Prince Max" (king, 1805) and his minister Maximilian von Montgelas, there was even more change. Governmental reform, begun in 1799, culminated in the issuance of a constitution in 1808. The Landtag, supposed to be elected by universal male suffrage, was never called. But there was a streamlined ministry, French-style bureaucracy, and courts. The Code Napoléon was adopted in part, and all of the French penal code.

The churches lost their monastic property and came under civil control. Freedom of religion was enforced. Mixed marriages (between Christians) were legalized, and Protestants were made eligible for public office. Jews, however, though free to worship, did not have full citizenship.

Legal serfdom and feudalism were abolished. However, peasants, even on secularized church lands, continued to pay some dues. Former serfs were entitled to part of communal lands (held by villages in Bavaria), but the distribution took years, and dues still were assessed by former lords. On "mediated" lands, formerly ruled by independent princes, the feudal system persisted almost undisturbed.

Centralization, however, proceeded apace. Local legislative bodies were eliminated. Cities lost their juridical rights and were administered by royally appointed mayors and police commissioners. A central Bureau of Education took over all schools, enforced mandatory primary education, and created some secondary schools. A royal bureau of health was created which improved sanitation and required smallpox inoculation. The metric system of weights and measures was adopted, and a bureau of statistics created.

Benefits were counterbalanced by the imperfect abolition of feudalism, increased taxes, conscription, and the operation of a state police, which, contrary to the law, applied censorship ruthlessly. Nevertheless, Bavaria made progress, and its constitution and laws gave promise of more.

RESISTANCE IN ITALY Italy, geographically speaking, was totally under Napoleon's control. Minor outbreaks occurred in the Kingdom of Italy, notably in 1809. Naples had guerrilla problems, but not for long. Marie Caroline sent assassins from Sicily after Joseph, but Saliceti's police literally met them at the dock. Otherwise, opposition came from intellectuals and artists, and it was mild indeed. So little did it concern the French that the classic pan-Italian work of the period, Vincenzo Cuoco's *Platone in Italia,* was published by Joseph in Naples. Ugo Foscolo praised Nelson after Trafalgar, but at the same time he was under pension and writing on patriotic themes for Eugène de Beauharnais. Perhaps the loudest protests were over the removal to France of Italian art works made by Canova and others. Again, however, most of the artists, including Canova, were serving Napoleon and/or his rulers.

Secret patriotic societies got their start in this period. The Freemasons, first and strongest, were initially pro-Napoleonic. Notably in Naples, however, they gradually became proponents of Italian unity. There too the Carbonari, originally a sort of "poor man's Masonic Order" got its start, giving the masses equal doses of primitive Christianity (Jesus pictured as an egalitarian) and liberalism. Nascent also, in the north, were the Guelphs, Federati, Adelphi, and others. None, however, generated any widespread resistance to the Napoleonic regimes.

The great intellectual heros of the later *risorgimento* were Vittorio Alfieri, entombed with great honor at Florence by Elisa Bonaparte, and Cuoco, Joseph's and Murat's protégé, who went insane in 1815. In the first "war of Italian independence," the secret societies supported Murat, who took advantage of Napoleon's return from Elba (1815) to try to make himself king of all Italy. (See pp. 165–166.)

OTTOMAN EMPIRE   Napoleon made unconscionable use of the Turkish empire to facilitate his schemes. He encouraged the Ottomans in their wars with Russia (1806–1812) and Britain (1806–1809). While he posed as friend of the Turks, he coveted their empire—if only as an avenue to India. His machinations served to weaken the already "sick man of Europe."

French military advisers, sent to Selim III in 1807 to modernize his army, were all too vigorous. A Janissary revolt resulted (1808) which ended in the death of both Selim and his successor, Mustafa IV, the last of his line. The army elevated Mahmoud II, who abandoned military reforms.

Turkey's problems encouraged revolts among the subject Christian nationalities of the Balkans. The Greek clans rose first and appealed to the tsar for aid. After Tilsit (1807), however, they turned to Napoleon, offering him, in small contingents, some 40,000 troops. The time never came, though, when he could profitably use them, since they wanted to fight the Turks.

Control of Wallachia-Moldavia (Rumania), at the mouth of the Danube, was the object of greatest struggle between Russia and Turkey in the period. Occupied in 1806 by Russia, it was returned to Turkey in 1812—part of the price of peace. However, Rumanian national sentiment had been thoroughly aroused, so that the Turks found extreme difficulty in reassuming rule.

The Serbs, led by Kara George (George Petrovich), rose against the Turks in 1804 and appealed to Austria for help, which was denied, however, by the timid Francis I. Kara George turned to the tsar, who was more than happy to gain an ally in the Balkans, the more so after French occupation of Dalmatia in 1806.

When in 1806 Russia invaded Wallachia and Moldavia, the Serbs were able to completely defeat their Turkish rulers and, in effect, won their independence. In 1807 Serbian forces operated with Russian armies in the south against Turkey while Alexander contended with Napoleon in the north. In December 1807 Kara George was declared hereditary chieftain of the Serbs.

Russia, however, was defeated at Friedland. A British fleet failed to take Constantinople, where defenses were prepared by the French General Horace Sébastiani. And at Tilsit, Napoleon talked of dividing Turkey between France and Russia, and broke the Russo-British alliance. Alexander attenuated his efforts in the Balkans and abandoned the Serbs, who were brutally crushed by the Turks and their savage Anatolian tribal allies, assisted by the Montenegrins. Kara George fled into exile.

In 1809, however, when the Russo-Turkish conflict flared anew, Alexander restored his support to the Serbian chieftain. Again the Serbs freed themselves. But again, in 1812, Alexander abandoned them to buy peace with Turkey. All his forces were needed to oppose Napoleon's invasion of Mother Russia.

For a second time (1813) the Serbs were crushed, but their spirit was not. Under different leadership they would rise again within two years to win autonomy. As in Rumania and Greece— which inspired other Balkan groups as well—the nationalities would never again live in peaceful submission.

HAITI In the early days of the Consulate,[1] Napoleon had plans for reviving the French Empire in America. Louisiana, ceded to France in 1801, was to be the breadbasket for the sugar-producing islands of the Caribbean. The chief of these was Santo Domingo, earlier divided between the French and Span-

[1] Surely, in part, influenced by his Creole wife, Josephine, born in Martinique.

ish, but all-French since 1795. We shall refer to the French, western, half as Haiti.[2]

Haiti's history had been markedly affected by the French Revolution. Following progressively liberal pronouncements of the National Assembly, whites first battled mulattoes (1790) to deny them seats in the colonial assembly, both sides using black troops. Then whites and mulattoes joined to oppose the representation of free blacks (1791). A slave rebellion ensued, the huge black majority finding leaders among slaves, free blacks, and some mulattoes. French forces were put on the defensive; massacres became common on both sides. Many whites and mulattoes fled the country spreading tales of torture, murder, and rape. In 1793, when Spain went to war with France, most of the black leaders took service with the Spanish of Santo Domingo against the French. The British sent help to the rebels.

In 1794, however, inspired by the egalitarianism of the new French Republic, Toussaint L'Ouverture, former slave, now a Spanish general, deserted to the French with his Haitian army. He rescued besieged French representatives and was appointed general and lieutenant governor of the island. An unlikely looking leader, small, wrinkled and awkward, he commanded respect by his intelligence, education—self-acquired— and iron will. To his aid came Henri Christophe, a massive, imposing black—illiterate but of superb dignity, taste, and common sense; Jean Jacques Dessalines, a raw-boned fanatic responsible for the death of hundreds of colonists; and Alexandre Pétion, a handsome French-educated mulatto.

Toussaint considered himself a Frenchman, but was determined that the blacks should rule the island. He soon expelled all French officials. That done, he negotiated a withdrawal of the British, who happily left the incredibly complex struggle. Toussaint then consolidated his control of Haiti and attacked Spanish Santo Domingo. In 1801 he was master of the whole island.

---

[2] The French referred to their part and/or the whole island as Saint-Domingue, a translation of Santo Domingo. Use of this term would be confusing, and French Saint-Domingue became Haiti in this period.

Toussaint L'Ouverture. The "George Washington" of Haiti. An ex-
slave who became a general and saved all of Santo Domingo for France,
he was betrayed by Napoleon and died in a French prison. Nevertheless
he had established the first black-governed state in the Western Hemi-
sphere. *(Library of Congress)*

Toussaint did not declare independence from France. He governed, therefore, unofficially, for France—and therefore after 1799 for Napoleon. A realistic man, he restored the economy by mobilizing workers, now free men, for the planters—black, mulatto, and white. In Spanish Santo Domingo, most of the original landowners had remained.

Napoleon was not a racist. In France, he encouraged mixed marriages. He had done so in Egypt, emulating Alexander the Great. But the massacres of the 1790s seemed to confirm the savagery of the blacks of the Indies. And the refugees and their allies had convinced him that the islands could be made orderly and profitable only by the restoration of slavery. He reestablished the old order in Guadaloupe, Martinique, and the lesser islands. Not so in Haiti.

Toussaint would undoubtedly have cooperated with Napoleon if left in charge of a free Santo Domingo. The First Consul gave the matter thought. In 1801 he credited General Toussaint with "saving for France a great and important colony," and said he deserved to be governor. But in Napoleon's eyes he was too independent. He decided to destroy the "black Washington."

He sent an expedition of 23,000 men under General Charles Leclerc (accompanied by his bride, the beautiful Pauline Bonaparte) to reassume control of the island. Leclerc carried a cordial letter to Toussaint from Napoleon asking his cooperation. His landing was opposed by the lordly Christophe, who burned Le Cap as he withdrew. But Leclerc won Toussaint over, and the other black leaders, their rank confirmed, submitted.

Toussaint, assured of Napoleon's friendship, trusted Leclerc too far, however. His reward was capture and transportation to France. There he died within a year in a dank dungeon of the Fort of Joux.

Meanwhile the black and mulatto generals became restive and suspicious. Rumors flew of the imminent restoration of slavery. Finally the betrayal of Toussaint became known. The natives revolted. Simultaneously fever began striking down the French. In September 1802 Leclerc reported that 100 to 120 men were dying daily, and that 4000 had died in August. He called urgently for reinforcements. In November 1802, Leclerc himself died of fever in the arms of his wife. Alternately hysterical and defiant, unwilling to desert other wives and the "cause," Pauline was finally forced to return to France with her husband's remains.

General Rochambeau took over what remained of the French forces, but Haiti was lost. Such garrisons as survived retired to the former Spanish side of the island. It only remained to be decided which of the native leaders would rule.

In Spanish Santo Domingo, the French were able to hold out until 1809. In 1808, however, when Joseph Bonaparte was declared king of Spain, the Spanish turned against them. A colonial assembly under Juan Sanchez proclaimed loyalty to Ferdinand VII, who was imprisoned in France. Indifferent to the rebel government which ruled in the king's name, however, they opened trade with the British and got military aid. The French soon surrendered. Until 1815, Santo Domingo enjoyed peace under British protection. In time, however, black rule would come to the Spanish side of the island as well.

Napoleon, grief-stricken at the death of Leclerc and horrified at the narrow escape of Pauline (who left behind friends who were raped and murdered), renounced further ventures in America. "Damn sugar, damn coffee, damn colonies!!" He decided to sell Louisiana to the United States (1803). Without the neutrality of the British, he could not continue anyway, and war with Albion was imminent because of his moves in Europe. (See Chapter 4.) After war began (1803), other French possessions in America were taken over at leisure by the British —Guiana, Guadeloupe, Martinique, and lesser islands.

SPANISH AMERICA   Napoleon forced Spain, once more, to join France against Britain in 1804. The British immediately cut ties between Spain and the colonies, but still found commercial opportunities limited. Briefly they considered forcing their way into Spanish American markets and in 1806 seized Buenos Aires, the capital of the Viceroyalty of La Plata (Argentina). But native opposition convinced them that negotiating with colonial leaders was the better course, and they withdrew. The colonists, however, had experienced the evident benefits of free trade. Moreover, under the leadership of Mariano Moreno, the *cabildo* (city council) appointed its own viceroy.

In 1808, however, after Napoleon seized Spain, Buenos Aires refused to recognize Joseph Bonaparte, as did all the Spanish colonies, and accepted a viceroy sent by the rebel Junta —Baltazar de Cisneros. His power however, did not rival that of Moreno. The *cabildo* at Buenos Aires, as in most capitals in Spanish America, though dominated by Creoles (American-born Spaniards[3]), loudly declared its loyalty to Ferdinand VII. It paid scant attention however, to the orders of the rebel government which ruled in his name (first a junta at Seville, later the Cortes of Cadiz, 1810–1814, and its regency).

In 1810, with the news of the fall of Andalusia—which made French occupation of Spain all but complete—and the flight of the regency and Cortes to the port of Cadiz, held by grace of the British navy—colonial governments became bolder.

In 1810 the *cabildo* of Buenos Aires deported the viceroy and set up its own junta of government; though still recognizing Ferdinand VII, Argentina moved toward independence. It grew rich on trade with Britain and all comers, except the French, plus the retention of gold and silver previously shipped to Spain. Expeditions to annex Paraguay, Uruguay, and the mining regions of upper La Plata (Potosí, La Paz), all failed. Argentina (the United Provinces of La Plata) nevertheless achieved lasting independence, formally declared in 1813.

In Paraguay in 1810 the wily Dr. José Gaspar Rodríguez Francia mobilized the gauchos and Indians and routed the invading Argentinians. He then formed his own junta and with enthusiastic mass support declared Paraguay independent (1811). In answer to the proposal that Ferdinand VII be recognized, he slammed two huge pistols on the lecturn; "That is my answer!" The revolution was permanent. Francia himself ruled until his death in 1846.

In Uruguay (the Banda Oriental), also attacked in 1810 by

[3] The Spanish-born were referred to as Peninsulars, or Europeans.

Argentina, the gauchos were rallied by one of their own, the square, tough, scar-faced José Gervasio Artigas. He too won his war, hands down, formed a junta, and declared independence. His government was destroyed, however, in 1816. Independence for Uruguay would not come until 1828.

Mexico (New Spain) exploded also in 1810 under the improbable leadership of a tall, gentle, superbly educated Creole priest, Father Miguel Hidalgo y Costilla. Until then the viceroy, General Venegas, had encountered no opposition. The Inquisition handled most of the troublemakers. These included Hildago, a teacher too interested in Indians, blacks, and "breeds," who was exiled to the remote village of Dolores.

In September 1810, Hidalgo proclaimed a revolution. It was doomed from the start. He offered no junta through which the Creoles could establish autonomy and raised an army of Indians, which to the white minority, Creole and Peninsular, was insanely dangerous. His program seems to have been more humanitarian-social than political. It proclaimed the abolition of slavery, and dwelt at length on improving the standard of living of the lower classes.

Moreover, he faced a viceroy who still had an army of regulars. His 80,000-man force was destroyed by royalist troops, and Hidalgo, hunted down, was stripped of his vestments and shot in July 1811, protesting his loyalty to his God, Church, and King.

One follower of Hidalgo would not give up, however—the Mestizo priest José Morelos, a burly ex-farmer and teamster. Based at Acapulco, he raised an army of peasants, proclaimed Mexico independent, outlawed slavery, and abolished most taxes. Until 1815, he held royalist forces at bay. When he was finally defeated and executed, however, New Spain seemed altogether its old self again. This was an illusion. Though not in the tradition of Hidalgo and Morelos, another revolution would begin in 1820.

Troubles began in Venezuela in 1810 also. The *cabildo* of Caracas, under Vicente Emparán, established a government avowing loyalty to Ferdinand VII, and sent the young Simón de Bolívar to England to seek aid. Destined to be one of the heros of Latin American independence, Bolívar in 1810 was merely an educated, traveled, young Creole aristocrat—tall, darkly handsome, and articulate. He returned with a famous native of Caracas, Francisco de Miranda, sixty, "El Precursor," ex-officer in the French army, sometime French prisoner, and exile worldwide. A professional revolutionary, he had tried to "liberate" Venezuela in 1806—with catastrophic results—and retired to England.

Caracas had not wanted Miranda. But once there, he took over and engineered another disaster. Rushing matters, he called a convention which proclaimed the independence of Venezuela (July 1811). Royal forces moved in, however, under Juan Domingo de Monteverde, supported by the ferocious Llaneros of the uplands. In 1812 Miranda, his followers scattering, was captured and sent to Spain, where he died in prison. Bolívar, however, escaped to Colombia (New Granada).

Almost simultaneous with the revolution in Venezuela, Colombia went into revolt. In July 1810 Bogatá, the capital, expelled the aging viceroy, Amar y Borbón, and called for a national congress. Most provinces responded, except Quito and Panama, which were occupied by Spanish troops. The congress, professing loyalty to Ferdinand VII, organized the United Provinces of New Granada under Camilo Torres. Bolívar joined him, helped him consolidate control of Colombia, and recruited men to recapture Caracas.

In 1813 Bolívar led an army into Venezuela through swamps and mountains, surprised Monteverde, took Caracas, and again declared Venezuela independent. Monteverde returned, however, again aided by the Llaneros under José Boves, whose troops committed horrible atrocities. By early 1814 the royalists were again in control.

News of the restoration (1814) of Ferdinand VII caused further defections among Bolívar's supporters and again he had to flee to New Granada. There however, royal forces moved in also and, despite efforts of Torres and Bolívar, reconquered New Granada. Bolívar fled to Jamaica, but his career had just begun. He was destined to become the liberator of Colombia and, with José de San Martín, Peru.

Chile also formed its own government in 1810, with the usual bow to Ferdinand VII. After vicious infighting among the rebels, a leader emerged in Bernardo O'Higgins, illegitimate son of the former viceroy. Liberal in outlook, a long-time resident of England, he was a Creole aristocrat who could please the landlords, who totally dominated the lower population. Unheroic in appearance—short, plump, and pinch-faced— he was nevertheless a fearless fighter and matchless politician. By 1814 he was *de facto* ruler of the state. In that year, however, royalist troops returned in force. O'Higgins was driven with his patriots into the mountains on the Argentine border.

There he was received by José de San Martín, in command of an Argentine army. Tall, rugged, taciturn, he had served in the rebel army of Spain, but deserted in 1811—probably because he decided an American (Creole) colonel would never get promoted. His mission for Argentina was to acquire western territory, but he resolved to help O'Higgins liberate Chile. This he would do, beginning in 1817, and go on, collaborating with Bolívar, to free Peru as well.

In summary, the only permanent revolutions of the period were in Argentina and Paraguay. Ecuador's (Quito's) revolution (1809) was crushed in a few months; Santo Domingo—excluding, of course, Haiti—remained loyal to Spain throughout, as did Cuba, Guatemala, and Peru. The control of the crown was restored in the remainder of Spanish America. The repressive policies of Ferdinand, however, would breed further revolution.

Spanish American independence in the end was more a product of Ferdinand's attempt at a total return to the old colonial system than the conditions of the Napoleonic era. Nevertheless the process got a strong beginning while the colonies were adrift, immune from Spanish leadership. The major heros of the later independence movement, all Creoles, got experience in this era. These men were uninterested in changing the social patterns of the continent. They made no effort to arouse the masses. But it was significant that the most solid revolutionary government, in Paraguay, was built on their support. Moreover the power of Indian-Mestizo-Negro armies raised by Hidalgo and Morelos in Mexico gave notice that eventually, and not only in Mexico, the white rulers would have to recognize their political importance.

BRITISH TRADE   Throughout the course of Napoleon's intervention in Spain, the British tried to induce the Spanish rebel government to open the colonies, officially, for trade. The rebels refused, though without British support on the Peninsula they would almost surely have been doomed.

This did not prevent the British from trading in Spanish America, but some officials were more than nominally loyal to Ferdinand VII. For example, Mexico only admitted British ships to carry bullion to Spain; Chile, in 1810, opened only three ports. Thus the British took negotiations with Spain seriously. Their first emissary was the Marquis of Wellesley (brother of Wellington), later foreign minister, who was succeeded by another brother. Neither reached any agreement. The final negotiations (1812) collapsed when the Spanish agreed to allow limited trade only if the British promised to use troops to enforce Spanish regulations. This bargain was refused, prefiguring the Canning policy which made possible the Monroe Doctrine of the 1820s.

The hypothesis that Latin American trade saved the British from destruction by Napoleon's Continental System is doubtful. Trade there was, beginning with the opening up of Brazil in 1808 (see p. 149), and the gradual penetration of Spanish America. But exports had dropped 25 percent in 1807. Thereafter the British overproduced for American markets, which were also tapped by Yankee traders. Moreover, Latin American buyers often did not pay their bills. As a result in 1810 five major British manufacturing plants went bankrupt, and others in 1811 and 1812. The British were further hurt by the curtailment of commerce with the United States (see p. 153ff). The result for Britain was an economic crisis in 1810–1812. The principal cause was overspeculation in South American markets. This period saw much unemployment in the British Isles, and disorders, including the famous Luddite riots, when workers smashed machines they saw as replacing them. The Continental System, therefore, was damaging the British economy, despite the modifications of 1810. But for victories on the Continent (Russia, Spain), the System might have had the effect Napoleon planned.[4]

BRAZIL   Portuguese America, meanwhile, fared marvellously. The government, driven from Lisbon by Napoleon's troops, was brought to Brazil (November 1807) by the British navy. The Portuguese royal family, headed by the Regent Dom John (João)—the queen, Maria I, was going insane—took up residence at Rio de Janeiro.

The departure of the royal family (November 1807) came just before General Andoche Junot's French army captured Lisbon. But it was not unplanned. Napoleon had announced that he would attack Portugal if it did not join the Continental System, expel the British, and confiscate their property. The regent agreed. He was not sincere, but meant to make gestures sufficient to prevent a French invasion. If Napoleon sent troops anyway, he was ready to leave. Essential government records and the treasury were crated; the ministers and their families packed to travel. A British fleet under Sir Sidney Smith stood off Lisbon. On the approach of Junot's troops, the court boarded ship in good order.[5] The impression of mad flight was given by the some 15,000 people who were not prepared and debarked helter-skelter, carrying what property they could.

Dom John's arrival was a shock to Rio. A city of 123,000, it was without sufficient housing and had no central water or sewage systems. Buildings, water, and sanitary facilities, as well

---

[4] See John Lynch, "British Policy and Spanish America, 1783–1808," *Journal of Latin American Studies,* I (1969), 1–30. More evidence for this is the increasing issuance of paper money by the Bank of England. Between 1804 and 1809 the circulation was around £17 million. It jumped to 19 million in 1809, 21 million in 1810, and continued climbing upward. The purchasing power of the notes steadily went down, whereas the price of gold, an indicator, increased—15 percent in 1809 alone.

[5] Smith also had contingency orders. If the regent remained to cooperate with the French he was to destroy the Portuguese fleet and burn Lisbon. Alan K. Manchester, "The Transfer of the Portuguese Court to Rio de Janeiro," in *Conflict and Continuity in Brazilian Society.* Edited by S. F. Edwards and H. H. Keith (Columbia, S.C., 1969), pp. 148–183.

as streets and lighting, all had to be supplied while many of the courtiers "camped" in the best houses available and complained.

At first the court spent heavily, to Rio's delight. But ultimately it had to restock its treasury. Taxes were raised, though Dom John made sure the affluent classes paid their share. Still, he was usually short of money for rewards and gave honors and titles instead, usually satisfying the recipients, most of whom were rich already. There was competition for offices between Creoles and Peninsulars, which had been violent before John came. The matter was complicated by the fact that most Brazilian Creoles—many more than in Spanish areas—were of mixed blood. The arrival of the regent, in effect, made them all "Americans," however, and tension between the groups subsided.

The British were immediately given trade rights, as were all nonbelligerents, though the British impeded American commerce in every possible way. Industry grew, as did agriculture, land and water communications were improved, the Bank of Rio de Janeiro was created; overall there was unprecedented prosperity. Iron industries were founded. Textile production saw an immense expansion; it would become Brazil's major industry in the nineteenth century.

The regent founded a Royal Institute, which, after 1815, recruited many Frenchmen. A Royal Library was established, and botanical gardens, which still thrive, in which the regent took particular interest. A naval academy and colleges of medicine and surgery were created. The first printing press in Brazil was installed at Rio.

Fortunately there was no question of war between Portuguese and Brazilian armies. The Portuguese had all along depended on local militia to control the colony. The regent created an army—but a native one—and continued to depend mostly on the militia. His regulars remained in Portugal to fight with the British and Spanish against the French.

The regent (King John VI in 1816), slight, needle-nosed, lethargic, but a winning personality, was a great success. His advisers, the Count da Ponte and José da Lisbóa, were well chosen. The latter, a disciple of Adam Smith, promoted policies perfectly geared to the needs of the time.

The king liked Brazil; Brazil liked the king. After Napoleon's fall he remained in Rio, propitiating the Congress of Vienna—which wanted legitimate monarchs back in their "proper" places—by declaring himself (1816) ruler of the United Kingdom of Portugal and Brazil. In 1820, however, Portuguese revolutionaries demanded he return or lose his crown. He went. In 1822, his son and regent in Rio, Dom Pedro, probably encouraged by his father, declared Brazil independent and himself emperor. The country would eventually be a republic, but not for sixty years.

THE UNITED STATES The United States had an alliance with France dating from the American Revolution. President Washington, however, at the onset of the wars of the French Revolution, declared the United States neutral. In 1793 he expelled the French minister Edmond Genêt for appealing directly to Americans and trying to equip French privateers in American ports. The French had not been too unhappy at U.S. neutrality; they expected to get greater value from the U.S. merchant fleet and the use of U.S. ports. But now the reaction was violent. And French ire increased when the United States settled its outstanding differences with Great Britain with the conclusion of "Jay's Treaty," in 1794.

A "Corsair war" began with French privateers and warships seizing American vessels and the Americans fighting back when possible. In the years 1797–1799 alone, the French took 834 American vessels. By the time Napoleon came to power, Americans, initially pro-French, were ready to ally with Britain.

President Adams decided, however, to try to deal with Bonaparte. He dispatched William Vans Murray, Oliver Ellsworth, and William Davie to bid for peace—with an indemnity and apologies from France. Napoleon, through his affable brother Joseph, asserted blandly that his government was not responsible for the conflict. He suggested that the "sister republics" just make a new start. They would cease hostilities, abrogate the alliance of 1778, and make a mutual declaration on the rights of neutrals, which by this time was becoming a hot issue in U.S.-British relations.

Charmed by Joseph, who brought in Lafayette and other

old friends of America to reassure them, and hoping to gain a lever against the British, the Americans agreed. A Convention was signed at Mortefontaine, Joseph's palatial country estate, in September 1800. The event was celebrated by days of hunts, balls, plays, and musicals. Napoleon and Josephine made a grand entrance, and the First Consul, playing the democrat, mightily impressed the Americans. Perhaps, wrote Vans Murray, he was too "generous" to survive in French politics!

The Americans turned to the problem of New Orleans, vital outlet for goods carried on the Mississippi. It was ceded to France in 1801, along with Louisiana and West Mississippi, by Spain. President Jefferson (elected in 1800) instructed Robert Livingston, minister to France, to try to buy it. "The Chancellor" (a former New York title) rich, refined, but big and studiedly "American," bid almost daily. Talleyrand proposed he should have a medal for effrontery, and at first denied that France owned New Orleans, then talked in riddles.

Napoleon had plans for Louisiana, as already noted. It was to be the breadbasket for the sugar islands of the Indies. He appointed General (later Marshal) Victor governor general of Louisiana. Troops and officials were assigned to replace the Spanish in New Orleans. Before the expedition could sail, however, its fleet was ice-bound in Dutch ports (1802). Meanwhile the debacle in Haiti became known. And the Spanish intendant in New Orleans, probably under orders from Godoy, canceled the long-standing American right to free deposit of goods (October 1802). The move was blamed, naturally, on Napoleon. The American frontier, by early 1803, was up in arms. Take New Orleans! War hawk senators echoed the cry. The president, to calm the congress, ordered 80,000 militia organized.

In these circumstances negotiations over New Orleans became serious. Talleyrand talked, assisted by the treasurer, the Marquis François de Barbé-Marbois, who had lived in Philadelphia, had an American wife, and was a friend of Livingston's. At this juncture, James Monroe arrived as Jefferson's special emissary. Once minister to France, he was remembered as the "American Jacobin" whose speeches had electrified the Convention during the Terror. Now forty-five, ex-governor of

Virginia and no revolutionary, he still had highly placed friends. Livingston resented his coming. Monroe, en route for London, considered himself part of a bluff being run on Napoleon.

Both were startled when suddenly they were offered all of Louisiana. Napoleon had told Marbois to sell New Orleans and everything attached to it. "Damn colonies!" The price didn't matter, but the more the better — cash.

War with Britain was imminent. French power was on the Continent. Louisiana was a liability; it was vulnerable to the British, why not let them fight the Americans (if anyone) over it? All to French advantage.

The Americans, prepared to buy only New Orleans and perhaps part of West Mississippi, wisely bargained for all offered. The price agreed upon, less some indemnities, was 60 million francs ($15 million). The First Consul thought he had done well. "Sixty millions for an occupation that will probably last a day!" he crowed.

When the treaty was signed (May 1803), his tune was different. "I have just given Britain a maritime rival which in time will lay low her pride!" Talleyrand was his old devious self. He refused to delineate the boundaries of the purchase — or even those of West Florida and New Orleans. "You have made a noble bargain," he said with a sly smile. "Undoubtedly you will make the best of it." Indeed the Americans would, despite troubles with Spain and Britain, which Talleyrand anticipated.

France returned to war with Britain the same month (May 1803). For a time the British tolerated American commerce with the French Indies, even accepting the "broken voyage" — Indies–United States–Europe — which "Americanized" French goods. In 1805, however, they cracked down and began capturing American ships. The United States tried to negotiate for protection of legitimate neutral rights, but the attempt failed, principally because the royal navy refused to renounce its right to stop American ships and impress "British" sailors. American naturalization was not recognized.

In 1806 British Orders in Council imposed a blockade on all ports under French jurisdiction, barring American merchantmen unless they "passed inspection." Napoleon replied with the Continental System (November 1806), and in 1807 declared fair prize American vessels complying with British orders.

The French again began seizing American ships.[6] Between 1807 and 1812, French captures outnumbered British 519 to 389. But the British began earlier, and their prizes were taken "nearer home." The royal navy often stopped ships and sometimes battled American vessels within sight of United States ports. Moreover, the British went in heavily for impressment of American seamen, which the French did not.

By mid-1807 the United States had good reason to go to war with either Britain or France—but American sentiment was anti-British. Jefferson, however, recognizing the weakness of American sea power, preferred a peaceful course. America's merchant marine was second only to Britain's, but its navy was almost nonexistent. In December 1807 he induced the Congress to pass the Embargo Act, which closed American ports to all but coastal shipping.

The president's plan, under his "little Continental System," was to cut off American food from France and Britain, and thereby force concessions. Britain did not lack food, since the crops of 1807–1808 were unusually good. But British merchants lost some £6 million in sales to the United States in 1808. Napoleon applauded Jefferson's action; it hurt British trade. He still, however, confiscated American vessels in French ports.

Americans became ever more restive, notably in New England, as goods rotted on the wharves and shipping companies went bankrupt. In March 1809, just before "Little Jemmy" Madison assumed the presidency, the Congress repealed the Embargo Act. It was replaced by the Non-Intercourse Act, which reopened trade except with Britain and France. Napoleon was less pleased: the British could easily conduct indirect commerce; he could not.

Both acts served to "protect" American industries, which

---

[6] Though a few had been taken between 1803 and 1807 by privateers. See appendixes of Ulane Bonnel, *France, les États-Unis et la guerre de course, 1797–1815* (Paris, 1961).

shot up to supply goods formerly ordered from abroad. Agriculture suffered a setback under the Embargo, but quickly came back, stronger than ever. The acts also served to delay a confrontation with Great Britain, for which the United States was ill-prepared. In May 1810, however, the Americans opened trade with both the British and French, with the reservation that if either lifted its blockade, nonintercourse would be reapplied immediately to the other. This could only lead to economic victory over both, or *de facto* alliance with one or the other.

In August 1810 Napoleon declared that the Continental System no longer applied to the United States. But, he said, only if the British revoked their Orders in Council or the United States could "make her rights respected." Big "ifs." The decree was a propaganda victory for Napoleon; the Americans, generally, did not read the "fine print." Public opinion in the United States became more anti-British.

The American government, though aware of Napoleon's "ifs," turned pressure on Great Britain. Nonintercourse, it announced, would be resumed if the Orders in Council were not revoked by February 1811. The British were responsive. There was an industrial depression; food was short. But they moved very slowly. Meanwhile nonintercourse was reimposed by the United States, and the American temper was rasped by incidents at sea, including a British attack on the American warship *The President*. Meanwhile, in April 1811, Napoleon, cultivating favor, unqualifiedly revoked the Continental System for the United States. The same year the British were "unmasked" after General William Henry Harrison defeated the northwest Indians at Tippecanoe and found the field littered with English weapons.

The news set off the war hawks in Washington, led by the youthful Henry Clay of Kentucky. The West was ready to fight. On to Canada! On June 18, 1812, war was declared on Great Britain. The British Parliament had already decided to lift the Orders in Council. But it was too late. The United States found itself an "ally" of Napoleon.

The War of 1812 was unusual in that negotiations to end it

began before it started and were completed before it ended. United States forces could not take Canada. The only American victory was that of Andrew Jackson's unbelievable collection of frontiersmen, French pirates, and local citizens arrayed behind their cotton bales at New Orleans. And it came on January 8, 1815, two weeks after the peace was made at Ghent.

The gains of the Napoleonic period for the United States were fabulous. Louisiana doubled the size of the country. Florida would soon belong to the United States. By 1812 the American merchant fleet was nearing the size of Britain's. The American navy, though still small, had displayed valor and developed élan. American agriculture and industry had "taken off," and banking and insurance expanded. Washington had been burned by the British in August 1814. But for robust, growing America this was only a ground-clearing for something bigger and better. The public believed the United States had won the war of 1812—ignoring British disinterest. "Old Hickory" had shown them at New Orleans!

THE WORLD 'ROUND Napoleon's machinations extended to Persia, where he sent a mission in 1807 under General Claude Gardanne to reform the army and gain an ally on the road to India. British influence, however, was too strong; the mission was expelled in 1808. Napoleon did succeed, though, in embroiling Persia with Russia for a time. Pondichéry, the last French station in India, had already been taken by the British.

In Egypt, meanwhile, Mohammed Ali came to power. He had fought against Napoleon earlier, but was much influenced by French ideas. Originally a Rumanian soldier of fortune who became chief of the Mamelukes, he was appointed (1805) viceroy of Egypt by the Sultan. He organized a French-style army, massacred the Mamalukes (1811), and assumed total control. He must be credited with founding the first modern state in the Middle East—reworking the administration, the judiciary, and introducing improved methods of agriculture and some industry. Until 1847 he ruled absolutely.

In 1802 Napoleon regained control of the Dutch Cape Colony (South Africa) held by the British since 1795, and re-

turned to Holland by the Peace of Amiens. The Dutch preferred his government, administered by natives, to that of the
British. But sea power told; the British retook the Cape in 1806
and retained it after 1815. They also seized Senegal (1809), the
last French outpost in Africa.

Napoleon, meanwhile, had established (1803) a French
station (Tamatave) on Madagascar under Sylvain Roux, for
trade and as a way station to the East. India was always on his
mind. But the loss of Senegal and the Cape undermined its use-
fulness. The British took it anyway (1810) and in 1810–1811 they
took over the remaining French islands in the Indian Ocean—
the Seychelles, Mauritius, and Réunion.

The last holdouts were Dutch colonies in the East Indies—
Java and minor islands. Ably administered by the Dutch General Herman Daendels, Java prospered, delivered occasional
cargoes of colonial goods to Holland and France, and fought
off desultory British attacks. Java finally fell, however, after
stiff fighting, in 1811.

There was no part of the world which remained unaffected
by Napoleon's passage, save its unexplored regions and the
ancient empires of the Far East.

CHAPTER SEVEN

End of the Eagles

RUSSIA In June 1812 the Grande Armée, 611,000 strong, was massed behind the Niemen in East Prussia and southward to the banks of the Bug in Poland; 130,000 more were in reserve. In glittering array, it reflected all the glories of a truly European empire, and showed none of its weaknesses. An international force, it included only 200,000 French, not counting 100,000 from new foreign departments. Every state of the Empire—satellite or allied—was represented, and there were contingents from Prussia and Austria as well. Most splendid was the Imperial Guard, 47,000 strong, an international army in itself. The Polish lancers, in grey and cerise, rode matching grey chargers; the Mamelukes, in silks and turbans, were mounted on Arabian bays. French, Swiss, Germans, Italians, and others in shades of red, blue, green, and white made a patchwork of color, gold and silver epaulettes gleaming, plumes flying.

Immediately available to oppose this mighty war machine were two widely separated Russian armies under Barclay de Tolly and General Pëtr Ivanovich Bagration, totaling together only about 220,000. It seemed "no contest." No wonder Napoleon and many others expected a quick victory.

But it was not to be. The Russians refused to fight when, on June 24–25, 1812, Napoleon crossed the Niemen, flanked on the south by armies under Eugène and Jerome. Even when the two Russian armies managed to merge,[1] at Smolensk, they quickly went into retreat. As Napoleon pursued them toward Moscow, however, the French army was depleted as he established depots and sent off units to protect his flanks.

On September 7, 1812, at Borodino, the new Russian commander, Field Marshal Mikhail Kutuzov, with the odds now relatively equal—some 170,000 each—made a stand. The battle was bitterly fought, but without a clear decision, despite incredible losses on both sides. Under cover of darkness, however, the Russians withdrew and, to Napoleon's astonishment, abandoned Moscow.

The French occupied the ancient Muscovite capital, which was set ablaze as they entered. They began by inglorious days of fire fighting, then weeks of monotony, broken only by desultory Cossack raids. Napoleon kept expecting the tsar to ask for terms, but he did not. French supplies dwindled; the army prepared to march west to winter quarters.

But the French emperor waited too long. As he began his withdrawal (October 18, 1812), snow began to fall. The horror of the next weeks need not be retold. What began as a movement back to supply bases—Vilna, and others—turned into a retreat which destroyed the army. Pursued relentlessly by the Russians, the Cossacks in the vanguard, those few thousands who reached Germany were haggard, ghostlike figures. They had lived like savages, sometimes on flesh cut from living horses so cold they

[1] The merger of the Russians has usually been blamed on Jerome, who shortly retired to Westphalia. But Davout seems equally culpable, if not more so.

could not feel the knife, and even from the bodies of their fallen comrades. Many of the physically fit had gone mad. But there had been legions of heroes, among them Eugène's Italian Guards and Jerome's Westphalians.

When Napoleon had gotten his men across the Berezina River—by dint of some of the most inspired maneuvers of his career—he gave command of the army to Murat and left for Paris. The emperor felt he had done all he could for the Grande Armée. It was imperative that he return to France—to raise new troops—but also for political and economic reasons. Always, when he was on campaign, there were those waiting for a favorable moment to seize power. A *coup* had already been attempted by General Claude de Malet. And the business community and general public needed reassurance as well. Napoleon's message: "The Emperor has never been in better health," has been cited repeatedly to prove his utter callousness and egomania. Nothing of the sort. It was the news all France wanted to hear.

Murat had shown great élan in the advance on Moscow. He was "back at home" on the battlefield, clad, as of old, in bizarre costume—Polish shako with egret plumes flying, Spanish cape, red boots, waving his famous jewel-studded gold cane; he never drew a sword. On one day he led twenty-six cavalry charges. The Cossacks so admired him that the Hetman gave orders to spare him no matter what. During the retreat, however, he became increasingly morose, fearing that Napoleon was finished, and even more that he would lose his kingdom to Caroline. He knew she no longer loved him and would take the crown if she could, even if it meant making a deal with the enemy. He began to think of making one himself. "Why not deal with the English . . . I am King of Naples."

At Vilna, where there were large stocks of food, arms, and ammunition, Murat refused a good chance to make a stand. "I will not be trapped in this *pot de chambre!*" The men looted the warehouses, and the retreat continued in even greater disarray. On January 16, 1814, at Posen, he announced his departure for Naples. Naming Eugène de Beauharnais his successor, without even pausing to brief him, Murat galloped away.

Eugène organized the survivors and garrisons in Germany

and led the army into positions on the Elbe, where Napoleon could easily reinforce it—a masterful military operation. The emperor was grateful. "My son," he wrote, "it pains me that I did not give command to you when I departed."

THE WARS OF LIBERATION Napoleon performed prodigies. By April 1813 he was back in Germany at the head of a new army of 170,000, augmented by troops from Jerome in Westphalia. Eugène sent more from Italy, to which he had returned when the emperor resumed command of the Grande Armée. Murat, repentant, returned briefly again, in 1813, to fight for Napoleon.

The Gascon, however, was soon back in his kingdom. Meanwhile, French troops were removed from Naples for service elsewhere. Murat was in complete control, and soon entered negotiations with the Austrians and British. His conscience bothered him, he wavered, agonized, wept, and delayed a final agreement. Caroline, however, prodded him on. In late 1813 he occupied the Papal States and Tuscany. In January 1814 he formally joined the Allies.

During the French retreat from Russia, the Prussian General Yorck von Wartenburg led his corps into the enemy camp. The Swedes, already allied with Russia, became more active. The Prussian king hesitated. In March 1813, however, after much fearful soul-searching, he issued a call "to my people" to support him against the French. His proclamation, however, was *not* a call for a national uprising. Frederick William was no man for French revolutionary methods.

Austria hestitated further, stunned by Napoleon's victories at Lützen and Bautzen (May 1813). The French emperor, however, agreed to an armistice on July 20, 1813. Meanwhile, in Spain, Wellington, who had temporarily driven Joseph from Madrid in 1812, defeated him decisively at Vitoria on June 21, 1813. He soon opened a second front against Napoleon in the south of France. Wellington's victory surely tipped the scales for Austria. To Metternich it seemed a positive signal that the tide had turned against France. Poland was already overrun— though Prince Joseph Poniatowski was with Napoleon—and the pro-Russian party was taking over. The diplomats of the Rhein-

Napoleon in 1813. No longer the wiry, energetic leader of men, he would yet direct brilliant campaigns in France in 1814, and terrify Europe with his return from Elba in 1815. *(The New York Public Library)*

bund showed much trepidation. Then too, Metternich, during the truce, had seen Napoleon's army. "Children" he called the new recruits—many age sixteen and seventeen—to Napoleon's face. And who will replace them?

When the truce expired in August, Austria joined the Prussians, Russians, and Swedes. The Allied armies won no easy victories at first. But after the great "Battle of the Nations" at Leipzig (October 16–19, 1813), Napoleon was forced to retreat to the Rhine. Behind him, his German empire crumbled as his former allies changed sides.

However, it is a myth that the German "War of Liberation" involved a great popular rising—and even more of a myth that liberal principles were important. It was a national war only for the intelligentsia who, later, however, convinced the Germans that it was real. Most of the troops who fought against Napoleon were regulars who switched sides on the orders of their monarchs. When Westphalia was overrun, Jerome was escorted to the Rhine by his guard; his troops, except for a few diehard Francophiles, then stood by, awaiting the return of their old rulers. The kingdom remained peaceful. His administrators and judges continued to function until removed or reappointed.

In Italy, Murat had turned coat, but his heart was not in the fighting. Pitted against Eugène, he did everything possible to avoid battle until Napoleon's defeat became certain, and cried unashamedly at news of the abdication. This did not go unnoted by the Austrians, who were given the fight of their lives by Eugène, who struck first against one corps, then another, and locally was actually winning. Nor were the British pleased, though represented largely by diplomats and military observers.

Napoleon, driven into France, fought an amazing campaign. Though his marshals were disaffected, his veterans jaded, and his recruits green, he won battle after battle. The spirit of the public was magnificent. But Allied numbers told. With the loss of Paris (March 1814) by Marshals Marmont and Édouard Mortier, it was all over. Faced with apathy and some treason among his trusted marshals, Napoleon gave up the fight and on April 11, 1814, at Fontainebleau, he abdicated.

On receipt of the news, Eugène, still fighting in Italy, made a truce (16 April) with the Austrian Marshal Heinrich von Bellegarde. Under its terms French troops left Italy, but Eugène's army remained intact and in control of the key fortresses. Earlier, the viceroy's father-in-law, Maxmilian of Bavaria, had urged him to desert to the Allies, promising they would make him king of Italy. Eugène had refused.

Even with the war over, however, it seemed possible that he might keep the kingdom. The diplomats at Vienna had invited him to send representatives to the Congress. In his favor were wide popular support, an efficient government, an army still standing, an excellent personal reputation as man and soldier, and the marriage connection with Bavaria. Against him, of course, were the Austrians, anxious to resume control in Italy.

With Austrian encouragement, minority political groups stirred up trouble in Milan. Rioting, in part promoted by imported "muscle," ensued. The Italian army commander in Milan declined to use his troops, and the Austrians asked Eugène for permission to move in and restore order. Worn out, ill, unwilling to foment more trouble for his people, Eugène gave over command (April 26, 1814) of his army to Bellegarde, and the Austrians took over. The viceroy, with his wife and family, retired to Bavaria, where he would live out his short life.

THE HUNDRED DAYS   Napoleon was consigned to Elba, and the Congress of Vienna met in festive atmosphere to restore "legitimate" government to Europe. But the Napoleonic period was not quite over. On February 26, 1815, Napoleon sailed blithely away from Elba. On March 1 the "thunderer of the scene"[2] landed at Cannes and made for Paris, his old troops joining him as he went. "Where is the man who would fire upon his Emperor?" At Auxerre, Marshal Ney, who had vowed to put Bonaparte in an iron cage, fell into his arms. On March 20, Napoleon entered Paris to wild applause; the rotund Louis XVIII had fled.

The emperor proclaimed a new constitution for France

[2] Lord Byron's words.

granting real power to legislative bodies, which were elected forthwith. He vowed to keep the peace and not try to expand his borders. Nevertheless Vienna declared him the enemy of humanity. Again he was forced into war.

The end came at Waterloo on June 18, 1815. Though the crowds of Paris howled for him to fight on, Napoleon again abdicated. The Chamber of Peers proclaimed Napoleon II (the King of Rome), but reversed itself under pressure from the Chamber of Deputies, led by the ingrate Marquis de Lafayette. At Rochefort the ex-emperor gave himself up to the British in the person of Captain Maitland of the *Bellerophron*. He hoped for exile in Britain, but his destination would be Saint Helena, where he died in 1821.

"WAR OF ITALIAN INDEPENDENCE" Murat, meanwhile, had performed what seemed an insane role at the time, but for which Italian historians would later glorify him. From Naples, he launched "the first war of Italian independence," against the Austrian armies in the north. Nominally, he was fighting for Napoleon, and it cheered him to so believe. Actually he was making a desperate move to preserve his crown.

Murat's kingdom was in danger from the powers at Vienna. He had given feeble help to the Allies in 1815. Metternich was his only defender, since he had made a treaty, though never ratified, with Murat in 1814; but he was weakening. The British favored restoring the Bourbons. Moreover, Wellington, the initial British representative, hated traitors on principle. Talleyrand, playing Austria and England against Russia in the French interest, cared nothing for Murat.

Napoleon's return from Elba fixed the attention of the Allies on Paris. Murat had an opportunity to strike at relatively weak Austrian forces in northern Italy. He moved while Napoleon was proclaiming his intent to keep the peace. The emperor not only had not asked his help, but denounced him to Vienna.

Murat, who had built his army to 90,000—though only 40,000 proved maneuverable—was assured by his advisers Maghella and Giuseppe Zurlo and other leaders of the Freemasons and Carbonari that Italians would rise *en masse* to join him and fight for a free Italy—of which he would be king. Caroline pled frantically that their only chance was to remain loyal to Austria. But if the Allies lost? "Napoleon will kill us!" she said, "I know him."

Murat went ahead with his crusade. At Rimini he issued a call to the people (March 30, 1815): "Italians! . . . Providence finally calls you to liberty; a cry which will be heard from the Alps to the Strait of Scylla and that cry is: The independence of Italy!"

Intellectuals came forth to make speeches and produce propaganda. But Italians stood stunned and left Murat and his Neapolitans to fight the war. Much to the king's astonishment, even Eugène's former officers did not rally to him. They trusted neither Murat nor the Neapolitans.

Wary at first, the Austrians discovered in a few minor engagements that Murat's army was badly led, disorganized, poorly supplied, and half the size they expected. Originally inclined to wait for reinforcements, the Austrians went on the offensive, easily driving Murat's forces south. At Tolentino, on May 3, 1815, what remained of the Neapolitan army, commanded by Murat personally, was routed.

The king fled to Naples, which he found about to be occupied by another Austrian army that had marched via Rome, and dominated by a British fleet under Lord Campbell in the harbor. Caroline had already surrendered, in effect, to the English, and was ready to go into exile.

The queen was startled to see Murat stride into the palace. "Do not be disappointed to see me alive, Madame," he flung at her. "I have done my best to die!" Caroline departed aboard a British battleship as planned. Murat became a fugitive.

THE ROAD TO PIZZO   Donning civilian clothes, he managed to reach France before the Waterloo campaign began. From Cannes he wrote offering his services to Napoleon. The emperor wanted nothing to do with him. The reasons are uncertain. Surely it was not because of Napoleon's aversion for traitors; he had recruited quite a number. Perhaps it was that Murat was a traitor within the family. Or perhaps, as General Bertrand says, it was because Murat had embarrassed Madame Walewska, the emperor's Polish mistress, who had visited him on Elba. She had been more faithful to him than any other woman, and he adored their son.

At this juncture, Murat, rejected by his emperor, deserted by his wife, who was deep in an affair with a general in Vienna, decided on a truly suicidal course. Sailing to Corsica, he recruited a small band of men and made for Naples to retake his kingdom. Publicly, he claimed that "his people" had always loved him and would receive him back. But to his friend General Franceschetti he said, "At least I shall die like a king!"

On Sunday morning, October 8, 1815, Murat, with about thirty men, landed on the beach near Pizzo. In uniform, wearing his unmistakable shako with its great plumes and diamond clip, he marched into the town square. To the people, many just emerging from church, he announced he was their king, come to save them from the Bourbons. Astonished, then fearful, the villagers helped a zealous local policeman capture the king's party. He signaled the capital, using the wigwag telegraph Murat's own government had installed. Back came the instructions. "The French general" was to be tried for treason. On October 13 a council, including some of his own former officers, gave him an all-day hearing at Pizzo castle. At 6 P.M. he was marched into the cramped courtyard, where a firing squad waited. Murat, vain to the end, gave the orders. "Shoot for the heart; spare the face." Ready! Fire!

At the time the incident at Pizzo was ignored in Italy. But in later years, as sentiment for Italian unification grew, Murat began to be viewed as a hero. Today the route of his disastrous march of 1815 is dotted with monuments to his memory, as is the city of Naples—and Pizzo. Even in dying, the last of Napoleon's kings planted seeds of revolution.

For the Congress of Vienna, busily erasing the boundaries of Napoleon's Europe, Murat's death only simplified problems.

Conclusions

*It is for me . . . for [the French] . . . to show the
civilized nations of Europe that they are one family,
and that the energy they expend in civil feuds
damages the common good.*
— Napoleon to the Corps
Législatif (1805)

THE REVOLUTIONARY   We have described the shaping of French institutions by Napoleon, the progress
of his reforming activities throughout Europe, the
counterreforms of his enemies, and his worldwide
impact. Beyond question, he was a revolutionary.
The extent and effectiveness of his efforts varied.
He sometimes compromised his principles; but
they never changed.

The nationalities, with British support,
brought him down—true—but under traditional
leadership. He had become a tyrant and committed
acts of pure terror—yet his regimes were more
benign, even in pacified areas of Spain, than those
which preceded or succeeded them. Thousands of
Frenchmen died in his wars; yet he had wide public
support even after Waterloo.[1] At the root of causes

[1] The myth is still prevalent that Napoleon killed so many

for Napoleon's downfall was his penchant for reform, efficiency, and change, which the French could accept, but other Europeans could not. To be the schoolmaster of Europe he had to become the drillmaster as well. It was because of this that the leaders of the Old Regime could use the nationalities against him. It is because of this, and his determination to unite Europe and make it self-sufficient, that the British kept up their steady opposition to him.

The Congress of Vienna was able to give the Old Regime a period of convalescence. But the patient would never fully recover from the blows dealt it by Napoleon.

We should turn, however, to the question asked in the introduction: Did Napoleon rule as he advised his son to rule? By his lights, he did. Despotic though he became, he considered himself a democrat—by Rousseau's definition, governing for the people. Yet he also granted constitutions to the states he created, dictating great parts of them himself. If in the end he gave the legislatures little or no voice, he would have said they were suspended temporarily because they endangered the Empire. It had to be preserved; without the Empire there could be no reform—no New Europe. If we can believe him, he meant, ultimately, to have all the constitutions fully enforced. But not until his system was secure.

As a proponent of equality, his record is good; of liberty, spotty. Yet the solid establishment of the Empire would have meant total enforcement of the Code Napoléon—basic to the protection of rights, the destruction of feudalism, and much else—in all of Europe, without qualification. Where he could truly command, the Code was enforced. Surely it is beyond argument that imperial French governments everywhere set unprecedented examples for efficiency and provided great benefits, even if offset by taxes and conscription, intended to be temporary. Napoleon safeguarded religious rights of all most

---

Frenchmen in his wars that the nation has never recovered. Actually only some 390,000 soldiers died—in battle or in hospital—between 1803 and 1814, inclusive, compared to 1,400,000 in World War I. Moreover, the population of France grew from 25,000,000 in 1789 to 30,000,000 in 1815. Total deaths, military and civilian, in 1814 were 873,000; the average for 1770–1784, when there were 20 percent fewer people, was 837,000 a year.

forcefully, including the Jews, to the point that he was accused of identifying with them. He even favored freedom of the press, but, as he wrote Eugène: "Everything should be printed . . . except obscene works and those which tend to disturb state tranquility." At Saint Helena he said the Code Napoléon, not his battles, would make his name live in history—evidence that he believed that he had been, above all, a man of the people.

THE GRAND DESIGN   As to Europe, Napoleon had a plan which went much beyond the vague "federation of free peoples" he spoke of at St. Helena. It was for a centralized state with common laws and institutions. Evidence for this can easily be found in the emperor's statements and actions during the years 1809–1812.

The abdication of Louis Bonaparte in 1810 and subsequent annexation of Holland to France are often treated as isolated events. They were not, and much more than Napoleonic economic policy was involved. The demise of Holland was to be followed by that of the other satellite kindgoms and probably lesser states as well. All the rulers were under attack. "I am creating a family of kings . . . or rather viceroys," Napoleon told Miot in 1806. But the "viceroys" did not implement imperial policy with the alacrity he expected, and he considered the nationalism they encouraged might one day be dangerous—even in docile Italy.

Then too, by 1809, he was certain he could father a son (he had two illegitimate ones). Nothing but a European empire would be good enough for him.[2] He proposed to remarry—a Habsburg archduchess—so that the heir, on his mother's side, would be of the highest and oldest European nobility. In late 1809 he divorced Josephine and in 1810 married Marie Louise. The expected son arrived in March 1811. In 1810, even before Napoleon had remarried, the boy had been titled "King of Rome."

Meanwhile, in 1809, harboring no doubts that there would be a son, he had informed Eugène that in 20 years Italy would

---

[2] The heir-designate had been the eldest son of Louis, who had never been formally adopted, however.

go to the King of Rome or a second son. This meant that the departments of the kingdom would become French. Napoleon's son's title would have been ceremonial, like that of the English Prince of Wales; he was not expected to rule. The Italian departments would deal individually with Paris and send representatives there—which would discourage national spirit.

Tentatively in 1809, and blatantly in 1810, Napoleon began his attack on the other rulers. Louis abdicated in July 1810. The Dutch departments were placed under Charles François Lebrun, the former third consul, but were to be prepared for individual administration from Paris. Jerome got exactly the same treatment as Louis. Part of his kingdom was annexed to France; an army, under the command of Davout, occupied the country, living off the land and even collecting taxes. Imperial customs officials entered to enforce the Continental System. The parallel was so obvious that Jerome wrote Napoleon that if he intended to annex Westphalia to say so, and get it over with.

Murat, in Naples, was publicly accused of profiteering in English goods and, rightly, of recruiting troops for his army in French regiments. In 1810 Napoleon let him muster forces to invade Sicily, sabotaged the operation, then blamed Murat for failing. In 1811 he removed all French troops from the king's command and forced him to dismiss nationalist ministers. In 1812 French troops occupied Gaeta, Naples' key fortress. Murat felt his kingdom in jeopardy, and it was. In Paris, Napoleon told René Savary, the new minister of police, that his son would have "all Italy."

In Spain, during 1810, Joseph was reduced to little more than prefect of New Castile. He kept his capital, court, and 15,000 troops, but most of Spain was put under marshals responsible only to Napoleon. Military governments were created in Catalonia, Aragon-Valencia, Navarre, Biscay, Burgos, and Valladolid—including Palencia, Toro, Leon, and Zamora. In Andalusia Marshal Nicolas Soult became governor without formal title. Between 1810 and 1812, therefore, not only was the war in Spain being directed from Paris, but its government as well.

Even in 1812, when Joseph was again given command of

the 300,000 French troops in Spain, there was no administrative reorganization. In fact, before he departed for Russia, Napoleon ordered part of Catalonia annexed "for administration only" to the French department of Haute-Garonne. The rest of Catalonia, still under a military governor, was divided into four departments under French prefects. The gradual annexation of Spain would seem to have been in the cards if the Empire had survived.

But for the challenge of the tsar (the Ukase of December 31, 1810), breaking with the Continental System, Napoleon might have gone further with centralizing the Empire in 1811–1812. The continuation of the process would have been quite natural. In ten years Napoleon had added twenty-eight departments to France—nine Dutch, four German, fifteen Piedmontese, Italian, and Swiss; the total was 130. In addition there were eight departments under military government—four in Spain, four in Illyria. Contemporaries commented on the trend. The Empire, said General Philippe de Ségur, would soon "no longer be France." True.

There was already, in fact, a European state, of sorts. Scores of civil servants of all nationalities, trained in the French bureaucracy, served on order in any part of Europe. The German Karl Friedrich von Reinhard, French ambassador to Westphalia, the Piedmontese Guiseppe Prina, and among Frenchmen, the Roederers (father and son) and Miot de Melito are good examples. Intellectuals such as Goethe harbored no narrow nationalism. Europe had an army: Napoleon mobilized it in 1812. Europe was also building a navy. Richard Glover has shown that by 1814 Napoleon could probably have matched the British ship for ship, or better. Whether he could have found crews is another question, but the British in 1812 were concerned over the threat.[3] The French emperor did not consider Trafalgar decisive for all time. There was not a "common market," but surely one would have evolved once Europe was politically integrated.

Napoleon's Europe would have been French-dominated

[3] Richard Glover, "The French Fleet, 1807–1814: Britain's Problem; Madison's Opportunity," *Journal of Modern History*, Vol. 39, No. 3 (September 1967), 233–252.

at the beginning. But in time, the foreign departments would have outnumbered the French.[4] Under the constitution they would have been authorized representatives. The legislative bodies were weak, but in time, with the coming of peace, could have been expected to take a greater part in affairs. A united Europe of all nationalities would have emerged.

If Napoleon had built a unitary European state, or even a centrally directed "Federation of Free Peoples," history would have been much different. It is difficult to see, for example, how the national wars in Europe, or the world wars, which began there, could have come about had Europe not reembraced the balance-of-power system in 1815. The dream of a united Europe, however, was not voiced again for a hundred years, and not forcibly until after World War II.

Historians have presented many theses on Napoleon's Grand Design—all with some plausibility. Some deny that he had one at all. But none, even the most antagonistic, can deny that he was a true World Figure, whose work is still influencing our lives.

[4] France had begun with 83 departments in 1789. Revolutionary governments had added 19; Napoleon 28. The addition of Spain to the Empire would have netted 32, Westphalia 8, Italy 24, Naples 14—and there would have been more.

Bibliographical Note

STUDENTS may get some idea of the awesome extent of Napoleonic literature by referring to the following, in order: Friedrich M. Kircheisen, *Bibliographie des Napoleonischen Zeitalters* (1902), expanded and published in French as *Bibliographie Napoléonienne* (1912), André Monglond, *La France révolutionnaire et impériale: Annales de bibliographie,* 9 vols. (1930–1965); Louis Villat, *Napoléon* ("Clio," Vol. VIII, Part 2, 3d ed., 1947); and Jacques Godechot, *L'Europe et l'Amérique à l'époque napoléonienne* ("Nouvelle Clio," No. 37, 1967). The latter two also discuss the past, present, and current direction of Napoleonic studies. These are the best bibliographies, but more are listed in Theodore Besterman, *A World Bibliography of Bibliographies,* 4th ed., 5 vols. (1965–1966). For recent works, one must refer to the journals. There are three major ones devoted entirely to Napoleonic history: *Revue de l'Institut Napoléon* (France), *Bulletin de la Société Belge d'Études Napoléoniennes* (Belgium), and *Rivista Italiano di Studi Napoleonici* (Italy). *French Historical Studies* (U.S.) and the *Annales Historiques de la Révolution Française* (France) deal partly with the Napoleonic era. More general periodicals are also useful; e.g., *The American Historical Review* and *Journal of Modern History* (U.S.); *The Canadian Historical Review* and *Bulletin des Recherches Historiques* (Quebec Archives); *Historische Zeitschrift* (Germany); *Revue Historique* (France); *The English Historical Review; Voprosy Istorii* (USSR); and many others.

Information on the documents of the period (beginning with the thirty-two volume *Correspondance de Napoléon 1er*) will be found in the bibliographies cited above. This essay will deal with selected secondary works (ordinary books), excluding articles, mentioning only a few new primary sources or ones in translation. Asterisk (*) indicates paperback.

Biographies

In English the best are probably Felix Markham, *Napoleon* (1963) and J. M. Thompson, *Napoleon Bonaparte: His Rise and Fall* (1952), which is less admiring and gives a fuller treatment. In French, Jacques Bainville, *Napoléon,* new ed. (1962), is authoritative and entertaining, though "true believers" may prefer Édouard Driault, *La vraie figure de Napoléon* (1928). E. V. Tarlés *Bonaparte,* tr. from Russian (1937), is a Soviet classic. Not to be overlooked are the older biographies of *H. A. L. Fisher (first published in 1912; paperback edition, 1967), and J. Holland Rose (rev. ed., 1923).

Life and Times

The list should be headed by Georges Lefebvre, *Napoléon.* 5th ed. (1965), English trans. in 2 vols. (1969); encyclopedic and laced with bibliography, it is admiring of Napoleon's talents but hostile to his empire-building. Jacques Godechot, Beatrice F. Hyslop, and David L. Dowd, *The Napoleonic Era in Europe* (1970) balances well against Louis Madelin's adulatory *Consulate and the Empire,* 2 vols., tr. from French (1934–1936). *The New Cambridge Modern History,* Vol. IX: *War and Peace in an Age of Upheaval, 1793–1840* (1965) has unassailable chapters on the Napoleonic period. The old *Cambridge Modern History,* 14 vols. (1902–1912). Vol. IX: *Napoleon* includes a famed bibliography. John Roach, *A Bibliography of Modern History* (1968) serves for the whole new set, and is disappointing. Martin Göhring, *Napoleon: Vom alten zum neuen Europa* (1959) sees the era as a turning point. Felix Markham, *Napoleon and the Awakening of Europe* (1954) and Willy Andreas, *Das Zeitalters Napoleons und die Erhebung der Völker* (1955) study the rise of the nationalities. Geoffrey Bruun, *Europe in the French Imperium,* rev. ed. (1957/1963) is an excellent short synthesis. Carlo Zaghi, *Napoleone e l'Europa* (1969) is a fine new contribution, if heavy on the Republic and the Kingdom of Italy. Among older works still useful for reference are Édouard Driault, *Napoléon et l'Europe,* 5 vols. (1910–1927), which perhaps overplays the "new Roman Emperor" line; the admiring, thorough, F. M. Kircheisen, *Napoleon I: Sein Leben und seine Zeit,* 9 vols. (1911–1934), though the one-volume English condensation is not recommended; and Louis Adolphe Thiers, *Histoire du consulat et de l'empire,* 21 vols (1845–1874), which is scholarly but very anti-British. Books that are good reading and filled with magnificent illustrations are J. Christopher Herold, *The Horizon Book of the Age of Napoleon* (1963) and Jean Mistler (ed.), *Napoléon et l'empire,* 2 vols. (1969), with text by a bevy of French experts; e.g., André Fugier on diplomacy and François Crouzet on the Continental System. There are many compilations of Napoleon's own words, among them J. C. Herold, *The Mind of Napoleon* (1955); J. M. Thompson, *Napoleon Self-Revealed: Three Hundred Selected Letters* (1934); and André Palluel, *Dictionnaire de l'empéreur* (1969). Of the spate of publications prompted by the 200th anniversary of Napoleon's birth, one of the most interesting is Jean Tulard (ed.), *Oeuvres littéraires et écrits militaires de Napoléon,* 3 vols. (1968), which includes his boyhood writings.

Youth/Brumaire

Books on Napoleon's early life rest on shaky evidence. Some of the more reliable, however, are A. Chuquet, *La jeunesse de Napoléon,* 3 vols. (1897–1899); O. Browning, *Napoléon: The First Phase* (1905); and Dimitri Sorokine, *La Jeunesse de Bonaparte* (1967); the least worshipful is Georges Roux, *Monsieur de Buonaparte* (1964). On Napoleon's accession to power it is hard to top Albert Vandal, *L'Avènement de Bonaparte,* 3 vols. (1907); though John B. Morton's *Brumarie: The Rise of Bonaparte* (1948) is excellent; and D. J. Goodspeed, *Bayonets at St. Cloud: The Story of Brumaire* (1965) is a solid popular account. For variety, one might see Albert Ollivier, *Le dix-huit Brumaire* (1959) for an existentialist view; and Albert Soboul, *Le directoire et le consulat* (1967) for a Marxist version.

Social and Economic Institutions

On Napoleon's reforms, Robert B. Holtman, *The Napoleonic Revolution* (1967) is superb. Jacques Godechot, *Les institutions de la France sous la révolution et l'empire,* 2d ed. (1968) is staggering in scope and detail. G. Poisson, *Napoléon et Paris* (1964) deals with the reshaping of the capital. On economic matters, much may be gleaned from works on the Continental System (cited under "Warfare" below) and Henri Sée, *Histoire économique de la France,* Vol. II: *1789–1815,* new ed. (1951); Claude Fohlen, *Naissance d'une civilisation industrielle* (1961); the first part of Rondo E. Cameron, *France and the Economic Development of Europe, 1800–1914* (1961); O. Festy, *L'Agriculture française sous le consulat* (1952); and the monograph of Odette Viennet, *Napoléon et l'industrie française: la crise de 1810–1811* (1947), which has broad implications. There is a paucity of social history for the period. Jean Robiquet, *Daily Life in France under Napoleon,* tr. from French (1962), is "social" in the everyday sense. More is to be learned from such as Régine Pernoud, *Histoire de la Bourgeoisie en France,* Vol. II: *Le Temps Moderne* (1962); G. Walter, *Histoire des Paysans de France* (1963); Robert B. Holtman, *Napoleonic Propaganda* (1950), which deals with more than France proper; André Latreille, *L'Église catholique et la révolution française,* Vol. II: *L'Ère napoléonienne* (1950); Daniel Robert, *Les églises reformées de France, 1800–1830* (1961); Burdette C. Poland, *French Protestantism and the French Revolution: A Study of Church and State, Thought and Religion, 1685–1815* (1947); R. Anchel, *Napoléon et les Juifs* (1928); and books on French art, literature, architecture, furnishings, dress, etc., for which Mistler, cited above, may serve as a guide.

Warfare

The classic of Theodore A. Dodge, *Napoleon: A History of the Art of War,* 4 vols. (1904–1907) seems now to have given way to David G. Chandler, *The Campaigns of Napoleon: The Mind and Method of History's Greatest Soldier* (1966), which should be supplemented by Vincent J. Esposito and J. R. Elting, *A Military History and Atlas of the Napoleonic Wars* (1964), which has the clearest maps and battle plans ever drawn. More dramatic is Henry Lachouque, *Napoleon's Battles: A History of His Campaigns,* tr. from French (1966). Lachouque's *Napoléon et la garde impériale* has been adapted and aptly retitled *The Anatomy of Glory* by Anne S. K. Brown (1961), who added scores of marvelous illustrations. The spirit of Napoleon's elite troops is perfectly reflected in the memoirs of Guard Captain Charles Parquin, *Napoleon's Army,* tr. from French and ed. by B. T. Jones (1969). Sir Charles Oman, *Studies in the Napoleonic Wars* (1930), presents varied subjects, mixing narrative with analysis of French and British tactics. Harold T. Parker, *Three Napoleonic Battles* (1944) has thoroughly mined the sources on Friedland, Aspern, and Waterloo. Robert S.

Quimby, *The Background of Napoleonic Warfare* (1957) establishes Napoleon's debt to the military of the Old Regime. A. T. Mahan, *The Influence of Seapower Upon the French Revolution and Empire, 1793–1815,* 2 vols. 14th ed. (1919), remains a standard work. For studies of individual campaigns, see Chandler's bibliography. We should note here, however, Sir Charles Oman's monumental *History of the Peninsular War,* 7 vols. (1902–1930), and its Spanish equivalent, Arteche y Moro, *Guerra de la independencia,* 14 vols. (1868–1903). For most students it will suffice to read Jac Weller, *Wellington in the Peninsula* (1962) or J. P. Lopez, *La guerra de la independencia, 1808–1814* (1947). Antony Brett-James (ed. and trans.), *The Peninsular and Waterloo Campaigns* (1968) brings life to events with personal documents, not surpassing, however, the horrors of his *1812: Eyewitness Accounts of Napoleon's Defeat in Russia* (1966). Alan W. Palmer, *Napoleon in Russia* (1967) is well written but unoriginal. Eugene Tarlé, *Napoleon's Invasion of Russia,* tr. from Russian (1942), is more analytical. Good contemporary accounts in translation are General Count Philippe de Ségur, *Napoleon's Russian Campaign* (1958), by the emperor's aide-de-camp; that of the soldier-diplomat, Armond de Caulaincourt, *With Napoleon in Russia* (1935/1960); and that of a later famous German on the Russian side, Karl von Clausewitz, *The Campaign of 1812 in Russia* (1843). Numerous accounts have been written of Waterloo. Of the newer ones, David Howarth (1968) and Christopher Hibbert (1967) lean mostly on British sources and should be compared with Henry Lachouque, *Napoléon à Waterloo* (1965); and for analysis, Robert Margerit, *Waterloo* (1964). On the economic war the new authority is François Crouzet, *L'Économie britannique et le blocus continental,* 2 vols. (1958), replete with charts and graphs. Eli F. Heckscher, *The Continental System* (1922) should not be discarded, however. An interesting new addition is John M. Sherwig, *Guineas and Gunpowder: British Foreign Aid in the Wars with France, 1793–1815* (1969).

Diplomacy

The most convenient, comprehensive, new work is Stephen T. Ross, *European Diplomatic History, 1789–1815: France Against Europe* (1969). He sees Napoleon as inheritor of expansionist policies initiated by Louis XIV and blames his failure on his harsh peacemaking. Shorter on detail but more interpretive is R. B. Mowat, *The Diplomacy of Napoleon* (1926). Unbeatable for erudition is André Fugier, *La révolution française et l'empire napoléonien,* Vol. IV: *Histoire des relations internationales,* ed. by Pierre Renouvin (1954). Herbert

Butterfield, *The Peace Tactics of Napoleon, 1806–1808* (1929) and H. C. Deutsch, *Genesis of Napoleonic Imperialism, 1800–1805* (1938) concentrate on the period when Napoleon's aims were still historically "reasonable." H. A. L. Fisher's *Studies in Napoleonic Statesmanship: Germany* (1903) still rates high, though weak on economic matters and anti-Napoleonic. E. E. Y. Hales, *Napoleon and the Pope* (1961) is as fair to the emperor as a churchman's work could be. Émile Bourgeois, *Manuel historique de politique étrangère,* Vol. II: *Les Révolutions, 1789–1830,* 6th ed. (1920), documented the idea that Napoleon saw himself as a new Alexander the Great and had a fixation on the East. His thesis complemented that of Albert Vandal, *Napoléon et Alexandre 1ᵉʳ,* 3 v. (1891–1896), that the emperor wanted only peace in Europe, but was blocked by Britain and the duplicity of Alexander. He in turn had adopted the ideas of Armand Lefebvre, *Histoire des cabinets de l'Europe pendant le consulat et l'empire,* 3 vols. (1845–1847), and Albert Sorel, *L'Europe et la révolution française,* 8 vols. (1885–1904), that all Napoleon's wars were in defense of the "natural frontiers" of France. This theme finds an echo in Driault and Bainville, cited above, and even in the early chapters of Georges Lefebvre. The changing ideas of the Russian tsar are dealt with obliquely in Patricia Grimsted, *The Foreign Ministers of Alexander I* (1969). Norman E. Saul, *Russia and the Mediterranean 1797–1807* (1970) is best on Tsar Paul I. A. W. Ward and G. P. Gooch, *Cambridge History of British Foreign Policy,* Vol. I: *1783–1815* (1922), is an old standard. Enno E. Kraehe, *Metternich's Germany Policy,* Vol. I: *The Contest with Napoleon, 1799–1814* (1963) should be compared with Heinrich Srbik, *Metternich: Der Staatsmann und der Mensch,* 3 vols (1925); G. de Bertier de Sauvigny, *Metternich* (1959); and Hellmuth Rössler, *Oesterreichs Kampf um Deutschlands Befreiung: Die deutsche Politik der nationalen Führer Oesterreichs, 1805–1815,* 2 vols. (1945). On the final peacemaking the classic is C. K. Webster, *The Congress of Vienna,* 2d ed. (1934). Harold G. Nicolson, *The Congress of Vienna: A Study in Allied Unity, 1812–1822* (1946/ 1960) gives less attention to Castlereagh, while Henry Kissinger, *A World Restored: Metternich, Castlereagh and the Problems of the Peace, 1812–1822* (1957) praises the diplomats who gave Europe a century of relative peace.

International

On Britain, one should consult J. Stephen Watson, *The Reign of George III,* Vol. XII: *Oxford History of England.* Owen Connelly, *Napoleon's Satellite Kingdoms* (1965/1969), deals with Italy, Naples,

Spain, Holland, and Westphalia, and has an extensive bibliography to supplement that given below.

ON SPAIN   Richard Herr, *The Eighteenth Century Revolution in Spain* (1958) gives the intellectual background. André Fugier, *Napoléon et l'Espagne, 1799–1808,* 2 vols. (1930), sets the stage for the French invasion. Gabriel H. Lovett, *Napoleon and the Birth of Modern Spain,* 2 vols. (1965), concerns himself largely with rebel Spain. Miguel Artola, *Los origines de la España contemporanea,* 2 vols. (1959), is broader in scope; his *Los Afrancesados* (1953) shows understanding of the Spaniards who followed Joseph. Ramón Solís, **El Cádiz de las Cortes* (1958/ 1969), plays down the influence of Freemasons and the mob on the constitution-makers. J. Chastenet, *Godoy, Master of Spain, 1792–1808* (1953) is journalistic, but not inaccurate. Geoffroy de Grandmaison, *L'Espagne et Napoléon, 1804–1814,* 3 vols., 3d ed. (1908–1931), is a most thorough work, hostile to Napoleon. Juan Mercader Riba, *La organización administrativa francesa en España* (1959) is a good short monograph.

ON GERMANY AND AUSTRIA   The best new work is Hans Kohn, **Prelude to the Nation States: The French and German Experience* (1967), which is strong on intellectual developments in Germany and Austria and annihilates the myth of a popular uprising during the "War of Liberation." Friedrich Meinecke, *Das Zeitalter der deutschen Erhebung,* 6th ed. (1957), is a good synthesis, though Joachim Streisand, *Deutschland, 1789–1815* (1959) is more abreast of recent scholarship. The old French standard, somewhat defensive, is Alfred Rambaud, *L'Allemagne sous Napoléon 1er, 1804–1811* (1874). Jacques Droz, *Le romantisme allemagne et l'état: Résistance et collaboration dans l'Allemagne nepoléonienne* (1966) emphasizes the role of conservatives in the resistance, Rainier Wohlfeil, *Spanien und die deutsche Erhebung, 1808–1814* (1965) studies the extent to which the Spanish "war of independence" inspired the Germans. W. Koppen, *Deutsche gegen Deutschland: Geschichte des Rheinbundes* (1936) resents the Confederation of the Rhine, while recognizing its role in unifying Germany. Arthur Kleinschmidt, *Geschichte des Königreichs Westfalen* (1893) is the most scholarly work available on Jerome's kingdom, though quite anti-French. E. Höltzle, *Das alte Recht und die Revolution: Ein politische Geschichte Württembergs in der Revolutionszeit, 1789–1815* (1931) and *Württemberg im Zeitalter Napoleons* (1937) are thorough and nationalistic. Marcel Dunan, *Napoléon et l'Allemagne: Le système continental* *et les débuts du royaume de Bavière, 1806–1810* (1942) shows Lefebvre's influence. C. Schmidt, *Le Grand-Duché de Berg, 1806–1813* (1904) is defensive in tone.

ON PRUSSIA   The older works, G. S. Ford, *Stein and the Era of Reform in Prussia* (1922); C. Lesage, *Napoléon I: Créancier de la Prusse, 1807–1814* (1924); and E. N. Anderson, *Nationalism and the Cultural Crisis in Prussia* (1939) are excellent. They should be supplemented, however, by R. C. Raack, *The Fall of Stein* (1965), which spotlights the reformer's domestic enemies; Walter M. Simon, *The Failure of the Prussian Reform Movement, 1807–1819* (1955); William O. Shanahan, *Prussian Military Reforms, 1786–1813* (1954); and especially Peter Paret, *Yorck and the Era of Prussian Reform, 1708–1815* (1966).

ON AUSTRIA   See Hans Kohn, cited above; Helmuth Rössler, *Oesterreichs Kampf um Deutschlands befreiung*, 2 vols. (1945), and W. C. Langsam, *The Napoleonic Wars and Nationalism in Austria* (1930).

ON ITALY   André Fugier, *Napoléon et L'Italie* (1947) is more scholarly but less exciting than Édouard Driault, *Napoléon en Italie, 1800–1812* (1906). R. M. Johnston, *The Napoleonic Empire in Southern Italy and the Rise of the Secret Societies*, 2 vols. (1904), is antiquated but useful. Emiliana P. Noether, *Seeds of Italian Nationalism, 1700–1815* (1951) is skimpy on the Napoleonic period. Albert Pingaud, *La domination française dans l'Italie du nord, 1796–1805*, 2 vols. (1914), is unequaled on the Italian Republic. On the Kingdom of Italy see Giovanni Natali, *L'Italia durante il regime Napoleonico* (1950); Carlo Zaghi, cited above; R. John Rath, *The Fall of the Napoleonic Kingdom of Italy* (1941); and Rath's sequel, *The Provisional Austrian Regime in Lombardy-Venetia, 1814–1815* (1969).

ON NAPLES   Jacques Rambaud, *Naples sous Joseph Bonaparte, 1806–1808* (1911) is definitive. Angela Valente, *Gioacchino Murat e l'Italia meridionale*, 2d ed. (1965) is sympathetic to the Gascon. It should be supplemented by Umberto Caldora, *Calabria Napoleonica, 1806–1815* (1960) and Pasquale Villani, *La vendita dei beni dello stato nel Regno di Napoli, 1806–1815* (1964) on economic matters. G. La Volpe, *Gioacchino Murat: Administrazione e reforme economiche* (1931) is still of value.

ON OTHER ITALIAN STATES   See G. B. McClellan, *Venice and Bonaparte* (1931), a solid study; Louis Madelin, *La Rome de Napoléon* (1906), perhaps the author's least worshipful effort; and E. Rodocanacchi, *Elisa Bacciochi en Italie* (1900).

ON HOLLAND   Pieter Geyl, *Geschiedenis van de Nederlandse stam,* Vols. VI and VII, new ed. (1965); J. A. Van Houtte (ed.), *Algemene geschiedenis der Nederlanden,* 12 vols. (1949–1956), Vol. IX: *1795–1840,* are both sympathetic to Louis, as is A. Duboscq, *Louis Bonaparte en la Hollande* (1911). (And see under "The Bonapartes," below.)

ON POLAND   Szymon Askenazy, *Napoléon et la Pologne,* tr. from Polish (1925) is friendly to the French; W. Sobocinski, *Historia Ustroju i prawa Ksiesta Warszawskiego* (1964) credits Napoleon with giving the Grand Duchy advanced law and institutions. Marjan Kukiel, *Czartoryski and European Unity, 1770–1861* (1955) gives astonishing stature to the tsar's sometime adviser. Abel Mansuy, *Jérôme Napoléon en la Pologne en 1812* (1931) comes close to being a history of the Grand Duchy while analyzing the incredibly complex situation prevailing there in 1812.

ON THE ILLYRIAN PROVINCES AND THE MIDDLE EAST   The following are useful: P. Pisani, *La Dalmatie de 1797 à 1815* (1893); Harriet Bjelovucic, *The Regusan Republic: Victim of Napoleon and Its Own Conservatism* (1970); M. Pivec-Stelè, *La vie économique des Provinces Illyriennes, 1809–1813* (1931); Vernon Puryear, *Napoleon and the Dardanelles* (1951); E. O. Ciragan, *La politique ottomane pendant les guerres de Napoléon* (1954); Édouard Driault, *La politique oriental de Napoléon, 1806–1808* (1904); Shafik Ghorbal, *The Beginnings of the Egyptian Question and the Rise of Mehemet Ali* (1928); and Georges Spillman, *Napoléon et l'Islam* (1969).

ON THE UNITED STATES   Good starting points are the diplomatic history texts of Samuel F. Bemis (4th ed., 1955), and Thomas A. Bailey (6th ed., 1958). Marshall Smelser, *The Democratic Republic, 1801–1815* (New American Nation Series, 1968), has a good bibliography. Good special studies include: Alexander DeConde, *Entangling Alliance: Politics and Diplomacy under George Washington* (1958), and DeConde's *The Quasi-War: The Politics and Diplomacy of the Undeclared War With France, 1797–1801* (1966); Ulane Bonnel, *La France, Les États-Unis et la guerre de course, 1797–1815* (1961), based on French archival sources with statistics on ship seizures; Arthur P. Whitaker, *The Mississippi Question, 1783–1803* (1934); Reginald Horsman, *The War of 1812* (1969); Joseph I. Shulim, *The Old Dominion and Napoleon Bonaparte: A Study in American Opinion* (1952); E. S. Corwin, *French Policy and the American Alliance of 1778* (1916); James A. Robertson, *Louisiana under the Rule of Spain, France and the United States* (1911); E. Wilson Lyon, *Louisiana in French Diplomacy, 1759–1804* (1934); Robert Tallant, *The Louisiana Purchase* (1952); George Dangerfield, *Chancellor Robert R. Livingston of New York* (1960); Dumas Malone, *Jefferson the President, 1801–1805* (1970); Adrienne Koch, *Jefferson and Madison: The Great Collaboration* (1950); Peter P. Hill, *William Vans Murray, Federal Diplomat: The Shaping of the Peace with France* (1968).

ON LATIN AMERICA John Edwin Fagg, *Latin America: A General History,* 2d ed. (1969), has lucid sections on the Napoleonic period. J. Saintoyant, *La colonisation française pendant la période Napoléonienne* (1931) deals largely with French America. On the Haitian debacle, C. L. R. James, *The Black Jacobins: Toussaint L'Ouverture and the San Domingo Revolution* (1938) seems dull compared to Faine Scharon, *Toussaint L'Ouverture et la révolution de Saint-Domingue* (1957), published in Haiti, and the dramatic, curiously anti-American Herbert Cole, *Christophe, King of Haiti* (1967); Ralph Korngold, **Citizen Toussaint* (1969) is a readable popular biography; Paul Verna, *Petión et Bolívar: Cuarenta años 1790–1830 de relaciones haitiano-venezolanas* (1969) gives hitherto unknown information on relations between one of Toussaint's successors and Bolívar. On more general lines, William S. Robertson's *France and Latin American Independence* (1939) and **Rise of the Spanish American Republics* (1918/1965) have stood the test of time. R. A. Humphreys and J. Lynch (eds.) **The Origins of Latin American Revolutions* (1967) is a valuable collection. Humphreys' *Liberation in South America 1806–1817* (1952) puts the French and British roles in perspective. More specialized are C. Prado, *Formaçao do Brasil contemporaneo,* Vol. I (1945); M. S. Alperovich, *Historia de la independencia de México, 1810–1924,* tr. from Russian (1967); Hugh M. Hamill, Jr., *The Hidalgo Revolt: Prelude to Mexican Independence, (1966);* and Simon Collier, *Ideas and Politics of Chilean Independence, 1808–1833* (1967). Among newer biographies, the following stand out: Augusto Mijares, *El Libertador* [Bolívar] (1965); Jay Kinsbruner, *Bernardo O'Higgins* (1968), in English; and Ernesto Lèmoine Villacaña, *Morelos: Su vida revolucionaria* (1965).

The Bonapartes

Frédéric Masson, *Napoléon et sa famille,* 13 vols. (1900–1919) has long been the standard work. Walter Geer, *Napoleon and His Family,* 3 vols. (1927–1929), is an adaptation of it. All glory goes to the emperor; his brothers and sisters come off poorly. This attitude infects the recent Theo Aronson, *The Golden Bees: The Story of the Bonapartes* (1964) and Margery Weiner, *The Parvenu Princesses: The Lives and Loves of Napoleon's Sisters* (1964). Readable biographies of Napoleon's mother include Monica Stirling, *Madame Letizia* (1961) and Alain Decaux, *Laetizia, mère de l'empéreur* (1959). Some studies of other members of the family include André Castelot, *King of Rome,* tr. from French (1960) and Octave Aubrey, *The King of Rome,* tr. from French (1932); Agnes Stoeckl, *Four Years an Empress: Marie-Louise, Second Wife of Napoleon* (1962); Constance Wright, *Daughter to Napoleon* [Hortense de Beauharnais] (1961); Bernard Nabonne, *Pauline Bonaparte: La Venus impériale* (1963); E. J. Knapton, *Empress Josephine* (1963); F. M. Kircheisen, *Jovial King* [Jerome], tr. from German (1932); Owen Connelly, *The Gentle Bonaparte: A Biography of Joseph, Napoleon's Elder Brother* (1968); G. Girod de l'Ain, *Joseph Bonaparte* (1970); D. Labarre de Raillicourt, *Louis Bonaparte: Roi de la Hollande* (1963); Prince Adelbert von Bayern, *Eugen Beauharnais: Der Stiefsohn Napoleons* (1940); Carola Oman (Lady Lenanton), *Napoleon's Viceroy: Eugène de Beauharnais* (1966); and Jean-Paul Garnier, *Murat: Roi de Naples* (1959).

Other Biographies

Also of interest are R. F. Delderfield, *The March of the Twenty-Six: The Story of Napoleon's Marshals* (1962); Crane Brinton, **The Lives of Talleyrand* (1936/1960); J. C. Herold, *Mistress to an Age: A Life of Madame de Staël* (1955); S. Zweig, *Fouché* (1930); Léon Kammacher, *Joseph Fouché: Du révolutionnaire au ministre de la police* (1962); Louis Madelin, *Fouché* (1955); François Papillard, *Cambacérès* (1961); Bernardine Melchior-Bonnet, *Un policier dans l'ombre de Napoléon: Savary, duc de Rovigo* (1962); Marcel Reinhard, *Le grand Carnot,* 2 vols. (1950–1952); Martha E. Almedingen, *The Emperor Alexander I* (1964); Vyvyan Holland, *Goya: A Pictorial Biography* (1961); and Hélène Colomba, *Madame Walewska: La plus belle histoire* *d'amour* (1964); Louis Garros, *Ney: Le brave des braves* (1964); J. B. Morton, *Marshal Ney* (1958); S. J. Watson, *By Command of the Emperor: A Life of Marshal Berthier* (1957); J. H. Marshall-Cornwall, *Masséna* (1965); Bernard Nabonne, *Bernadotte* (1946); Carola Oman, *Nelson* (1954) and *Sir John Moore* (1953); Elizabeth, Lady Longford, *Wellington: The Years of the Sword* (1960); and Michael Glover, *Wellington as Military Commander* (1968).

The Last Days

On Napoleon's downfall in 1813–1814, see the diplomatic and military histories and the classic Henri Houssaye, *1814* (1888). On a domestic crisis of 1812: Guido Artom, *Napoleon is Dead in Russia: The Extraordinary Story of one of History's Strangest Conspiracies* (1970), and the more factual B. Melchoir-Bonnet, *La conspiration du général Malet* (1963). On the first exile: Robert Christophe, *Napoléon on Elba*, tr. from French (1964), and G. Godlewski, *Trois-cents jours d'exil: Napoléon à l'Île d'Elbe* (1961). On Napoleon's return: Henry Lachouque, *The Last Days of Napoleon's Empire: From Waterloo to Saint Helena*, tr. from French (1966), Henri Houssaye, *1815*, 3 vols. (1898–1925); Edith Saunders, *The Hundred Days* (1963); Emanuelle Hubert, *Les cents jours* (1966); Ray E. Chubberly, *The Role of Fouché during the Hundred Days* (1969); Michael J. Thornton, *Napoleon after Waterloo: England and the Saint Helena Decision* (1968); Jean Duhamel, *The Fifty Days: Napoleon in England*, tr. from French (1970). On Saint Helena, see Gilbert Martineau, *Napoleon's Saint Helena* (1969) and R. Korngold, *The Last Years of Napoleon* (1959). A. P. Primrose, Lord Rosebery, *Napoleon: The Last Phase* (1900) deserves special notice for its criticism of the Saint Helena literature and comments on its writers, and is a literary masterpiece. Many firsthand accounts concerning Napoleon in exile are available in English, including those of Barry O'Meara, Emmanuel de Las Casas, and Generals Montholon and Gourgaud. The most recent addition is *Napoleon at Saint Helena* (1962) extracted from General Henri Bertrand, *Cahiers de Sainte-Hélène*, 3 vols., deciphered and edited by Paul Fleuriot de Langle (1949–1959). Napoleon's health and the cause of his death have remained a source of fascination. Sten Forshufvud, a Swedish dentist, in *Who Murdered Napoleon?* (1961) resurrects the discredited arsenic-poisoning story. Dr. James Kemble, *Napoleon Immortal: The Medical History and Private Life of Napoleon Bonaparte* (1959) opts on good grounds for stomach ulcers and/or cancer.

Historiography

Pieter Geyl, *Napoleon: For and Against* (1949) analyzes the writings of French historians and writers on Napoleon. Albert Guérard, *Reflections on the Napoleonic Legend* (1924) sounds a vitriolic note. David H. Pinckney (ed.), *Napoleon: Historical Enigma* (1969) presents excerpts from the works of eighteen authors. Jean Tulard (ed.), *L'Anti-Napoléon: La légende noire de l'empéreur* (1965) presents unfavorable writings with often devastating commentary. J. Lucas-Dubreton, *Le culte de Napoléon, 1814–1848* (1960) is a synthesis. H. A. L. Fisher's erudite *Bonapartism* (1908) is evenhanded but anti-Napoleonic. Godechot's bibliography (*L'Époque Napoléonienne*, 1967), cited above, has a fine "For or Against" chapter.

Index